COUP

COUP

REFLECTIONS ON THE POLITICAL CRISIS IN FIJI

EDITORS
BRIJ V. LAL with MICHAEL PRETES

ANU

THE AUSTRALIAN NATIONAL UNIVERSITY

E PRESS

ANU

E PRESS

Published by ANU E Press
The Australian National University
Canberra ACT 0200, Australia
Email: anuepress@anu.edu.au

Previously published by Pandanus Books

National Library in Australia Cataloguing-in-Publication entry

Title: Coup : reflections on the political crisis in Fiji /
             editors, Brij V. Lal ; Michael Pretes.

ISBN: 9781921536366 (pbk.)

             9781921536373 (pdf)

Notes: Bibliography.

Subjects: Fiji--Politics and government.

Other Authors/Contributors:

             Lal, Brij V.
             Pretes, Michael, 1963-

Dewey Number: 320.99611

ACKNOWLEDGEMENTS

Many of the papers in this collection previously appeared in newspapers and magazines, and as internet postings at the height of Fiji's political crisis between May and June 2000. We thank the authors of these contributions for permission to reprint their writings. We also thank the journals, magazines, and web sites themselves for allowing us to reprint these contributions: *Pacific World, The Listener, Fiji Times, Sydney Morning Herald, Canberra Times, The Australian, The Independent* (UK), Pacific Journalism Online, Fijilive.com, *Eureka Street, Daily Post,* Pacific Island Network, *Pacific Economic Bulletin, Journal of South Pacific Law,* and Te Karere Ipurangi. Ross Himona, of Te Karere Ipurangi, and David Robie, of the University of the South Pacific's Journalism Online program, were of particular assistance in tracking down contributors. Ian Templeman and his staff at Pandanus Books also deserve thanks for their assistance towards the completion of this project. Annette Craig at the Centre for the Contemporary Pacific helped with the final preparation of the manuscript.

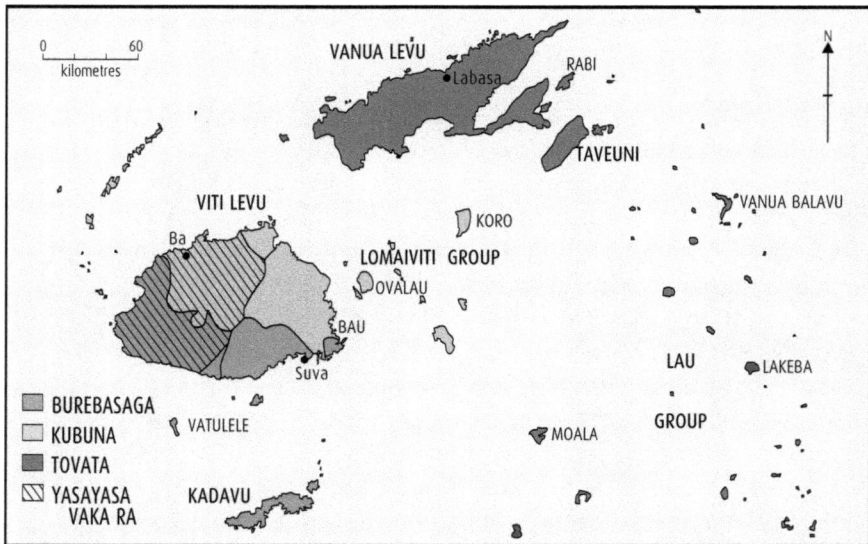

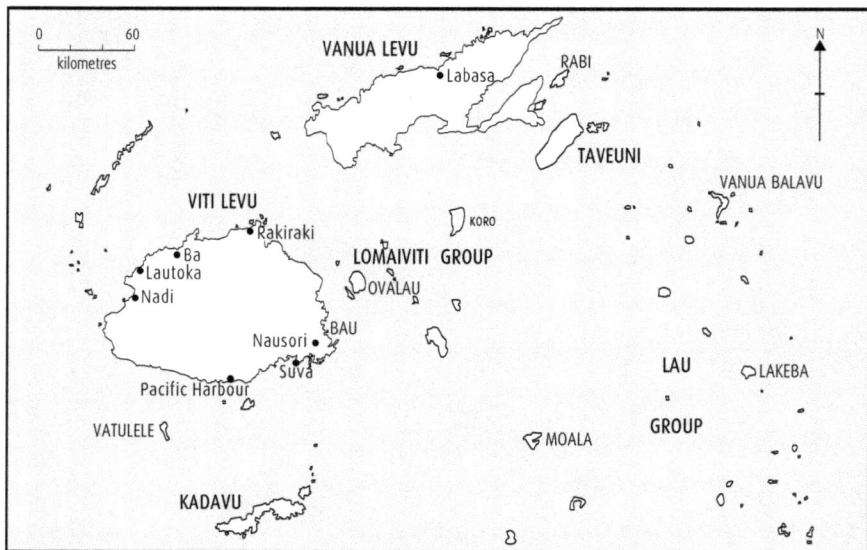

CONTENTS

PREFACE

In the *Eighteenth Brumaire of Louis Napoleon*, Marx remarks that history repeats itself, so to speak, twice: the first time as tragedy, the second as farce. The events in Fiji of May–July 2000 would tend to exemplify this dictum. One coup is bad enough, but three in thirteen years staggers the imagination.

This collection is not an academic analysis of these events, their origins, processes and impacts. Rather, the contributors to this volume simply reflect, often in the heat of the moment, on what the coup meant to them. The contributors are Fijians of all stripes as well as others who take an interest in the country. They express themselves in statements, speeches, essays and laments.

Many overseas people familiar with Fiji are dismayed and disillusioned with the events in that country. Many contribute pieces to newspapers or the internet. The majority are critical, praying for an early resolution of the crisis. They are moving in their sincerity, eloquent and anguished in their tone. This volume of essays contains a sample, but only a small sample, of these responses. They were written when the Fiji crisis was in full swing. The hostages were still in the parliamentary complex, and George Speight was a regular sight on our television screens. Since then, academic analyses have appeared, focusing on the larger political and electoral issues that underpinned the crisis. More will assuredly come as the dust settles and people attempt to make sense of the madness that so dramatically engulfed their lives.

Editors inspect what they get, not get what they expect, a colleague reminded us as we grappled with the balance of perspective reflected in this collection. As it happens, the overwhelming bulk of the published commentary on the Fijian crisis was critical of the events. Our effort to solicit contrary perspectives was not as fruitful as we would have liked. This is regrettable, but that is the way things are. There is enough here to give the reader a fair sense of the issues on all sides of the political divide.

The strength of this collection lies in its contemporaneity, catching unprocessed voices as the events were unfolding in Fiji. Many pieces are straight from the heart, expressing bewilderment, frustration, anger and anguish. They are partial, in both senses of the word. As they have to be. Nonetheless, they will form an indispensable building block of a future interpretative edifice. The collection is offered to the readers in that spirit.

Brij V. Lal and Michael Pretes
May 2001

FIJICOUP.COM

Brij V. Lal

I met Bruce Hill only recently, but I feel I have known him for a long time. Now managing a public radio station in Melbourne, Bruce was for many years with Radio New Zealand's Pacific program. Once a month or so, he would ring me to talk about Fiji, get my assessment of the situation there, pass on anecdotal information he had. Our talk would be interspersed with banter and political gossip. So, when he rang me around 9:30am on 19 May, I expected another casual conversation about Fiji. 'Have you heard?' he asked. I hadn't. 'Some thugs have marched into Parliament and hijacked the government.' That was all he knew, but promised to get back soon.

I headed straight to the Fiji High Commission, whose own phone bank was clogged with callers, mostly Fiji people living in Australia. They had heard a brief report on the morning radio. The High Commissioner, Ratu Isoa Gavidi, an urbane man of moderate views, was as non-plussed as I was, though not his deputy R_siate Korovusere, who would later be remanded in custody for openly supporting the coup leader, George Speight. Over cups of tea we measured our concern, and waited for more news. Nothing came. We then decided to ring the Australian Foreign Affairs Department whose secure communication links with Suva provided more detail. Ten armed men, of unknown identity, had taken the Prime Minister hostage, perhaps the Parliament itself. That was all they knew.

By the time I returned to my office around midday, concerned colleagues were milling in the corridors outside my office, wanting more information, expressing sympathy, shaking their heads in bewildered frustration, most knowing that a major part of my life's work faced the danger of premature derailment.

Fijilive is — and has been for sometime — our lifeline to Fiji. This is new: there was no internet in 1987, the time of the first two coups. Fiji's unfolding drama was being relayed to the world in real time. The internet is the great democratiser: everyone is reading the same text, the same background pieces, important documents and policy speeches. Many of these sources would disappear from the screen within a week or so, lost, I suspect, to future researchers. The first announcement of the Fiji crisis comes from Fijilive: 'Seven civilians armed with AK-47s have locked the Prime Minister and Cabinet Ministers in the upper chamber of Fiji's Parliament. One man is standing at the gate and not letting anyone in. Some shots were fired but it is not clear at this stage whether anyone is hurt.' Those words brought back to my mind what I had heard in 1987. Words fail to describe my sense of anguish and disappointment.

More news comes later. Readers are informed of the long-planned violence-threatening protest march organised by the recently revived Taukei Movement to present a petition to the President against the People's Coalition government. Groups of Fijian men and women are reported rejoicing, dancing to the tune of reggae music blaring from specially hired trucks. Later that afternoon, a rough, rag tag band of Fijian youth, returning from the parliamentary complex at Vieuto, rampages across central Suva, stoning shop windows, trashing the streets. Police are nowhere in sight. Fear and panic seize the city as people clear out of Suva in overflowing taxis and buses. The scene is reminiscent of 1987, except that it is much worse this time.

As night descends on an empty, frightened city, the place erupts. Drunken hooligans take matters into their own hands, looting and torching shops. The looting continues well into the night. Whole families are caught on camera helping themselves, picking and choosing clothes, toys, television sets, cameras, carting their loot in trolleys, on their shoulders, in vans. The image of a young Fijian boy in the back of a pickup van, grinning at the camera, with a large television set wobbly on his knees, lingers in the mind. 'Family shopping' is what one man cheerfully tells a foreign reporter. Suva is covered in black smoke, its streets littered with broken glass and discarded damaged goods. Grieving, distraught shop owners weep amidst the charred remains of their life's work. Shops will be re-built and shelves will once again be re-stocked, but the memory of terror and pillage will scar their lives forever.

For the next few weeks, attention shifts to the carnival atmosphere at the parliamentary complex. Women singing and dancing, people sitting on mats clapping, drinking *yaqona*, the blue smoke from *lovo* fires, young men and women loitering, the terrorising of foreign journalists by coup supporters. Commentators overseas express bewilderment at the apparent ease with which coup supporters breach the security cordon set up by the military. There is open speculation about the complicity of the police and the army in the unfolding mayhem. The army is divided, the police force strangely disabled. George Speight, brightly dressed, wearing a permanent smirk on his face, his bald pate shining in the camera lights, holds forth regularly about his mission. He is bantering, slick, a salesman; but his gift of the gab also jars, his pronouncements lacking conviction and authority. He is no Rabuka. He is, in fact, his own worst enemy.

Eager to stage its own coup, my university alerts the media to my presence as a Fiji expert, a co-architect of the 1997 Fiji Constitution. ABC's *Midday Show* is the first to call, seeking an instant take on the unfolding events. Is it a coup? No, I say, this is not 1987. The army is still in the barracks, and no recognisable group has claimed credit for the deed. It is a hijack of Parliament, I say, the crisis likely to be over by the weekend. Surely the lessons of 1987 had been learned. No one in their right mind, I ventured, would like to revisit that dark period, from which the country was just beginning to recover. How wrong I turned out to be. Historians are better at predicting the past than divining the future.

Who was George Speight? Did I know him, or of him? I did, I said. I had met him in 1997 when my fellow Constitution Commissioner, Tomasi Vakatora, and I had gone to Brisbane to explain to the Fiji community there the essence of our report. After the talk, Speight, athletic, articulate, grinning, had embraced me and said, 'Doc, this is a brilliant report. The only thing wrong with it is that you did not recommend dual citizenship.' I later realised the self-interest that prompted his remark. Speight, living in Australia, wanted to have it both ways. I was not against the idea,

I responded, but it had to apply to all Fiji citizens, not only to the indigenous community, as some Fijian submissions demanded. Padma, my wife, was likewise impressed with Speight, his command of the English language, his presence and his vision for Fiji. 'If only we had more people like him, Fiji would be a much better place,' she mused.

Trying to understand his background, some people in the media began calling George Speight a 'global businessman'. This was in reference to his reported business activity in several countries. I called Speight a 'failed businessman', and that description stuck. I was not wrong or malicious. Speight had left behind him, wherever he had worked, a path littered with broken promises, failed deals, shady transactions. I was later to learn that although well connected and with powerful patrons in the Rabuka government, Speight had been dumped as chairman of both the Fiji Pine and the Hardwood Corporations. Personal and pecuniary interests, rather more than a well-defined political philosophy, drove Speight. He was the front man for an assortment of other interests, I told the media, defeated politicians, ultranationalists, the riders of the gravy trains of the 1990s now facing the prospect of public scrutiny.

The ABC interview, done while the gun was still smoking, opened the floodgate. Radio stations from around the country, as well as overseas, called, many several times and at odd hours. Some asked probing questions, but most sought elementary information about Fiji, its politics, demography, the 1997 Constitution. The commercial radio and television stations were cashing in on an unfolding story, highlighting the dramatic, seeking my quick take on the events, seeing Fiji through the prism of their own prejudices or understandings of 'indigenous' and other such issues. Live interviews on commercial stations are a dangerous terrain. The presenters ask questions but then put their own 'spin' on my answers, sometimes imposing interpretations on one's words beyond what had been said or intended. But it is too late to correct: the presenters move on to other pressing issues of the day. Over time, though, I learn to 'play' the media better, using their questions to get my own points across.

The newspaper coverage is different. Unlike 1987, there is by and large a better, more complex, nuanced, understanding of the issues in Fiji.

The Fijian crisis is no longer portrayed solely as a racial issue. This crisis, we learn, is more about a fight for power and political supremacy among various groups of indigenous Fijians, in which Indo-Fijians are used as a scapegoat. Speight's real target is the eastern hierarchy represented by Ratu Mara about whom Speight is openly disparaging. This was once unthinkable. The 1987 coup was believable as an indigenous uprising against a government dominated by Indo-Fijians. Speight's coup is an uprising against an experiment that was working, against a Constitution blessed by the Great Council of Chiefs and unanimously approved by a Parliament dominated by indigenous Fijians. Often there is open sympathy for the Indo-Fijians among many reporters who know that all the guns are on the other side, a people whose only crime is their success achieved through decades of hard work.

Several major Australian newspapers have their own reporters on the ground. Unlike the television journalists who set their sights on the besieged parliamentary complex, presenting a distorted picture about what was actually happening in the country at large, the newspaper reporters go beyond Suva to the countryside, focusing on the plight of people terrorised by Speight's supporters. They write about the harrowing human casualties of the tragedy. The pictures of burnt tin shacks, of people weeping as they pick up the pieces, of frightened shopkeepers seeking shelter behind shuttered windows, of menacing young men armed with knives and sticks ready to go on a rampage, leave behind unsettling images that continue to haunt.

Another difference between 1987 and 2000 is the advent of the internet. Ten years ago, the facsimile machine was the latest communication invention, revolutionary and mind-boggling in the speed with which information could be conveyed. But the internet is something else, enabling people to follow up the breaking story in real time. Even Speight, we learn, browses through the internet as he prepares for the day's interviews. Fijilive is the main source of information, interviews, documents, indispensable to lay readers and professionals alike. Other sites spring up in Hawaii, Vancouver, Auckland and Sydney, carrying stories, opinion pieces and editorials from around the world. Chat sites mushroom, enabling people with assumed names from around the globe to express their thoughts and opinions, vent their frustration and anger, engage in racial abuse.

I begin to realise for the first time how truly wired-up the world is. There is information overload. The real challenge is to make sense of this mass of information, constructing a coherent, contextualised picture. And that is where my expertise as a historian comes into play. I have been engaged in research on Fijian history and politics for two decades now, more recently as a participant in its constitutional developments. That knowledge base, built up over a long period, and informed by frequent visits to the country and an acquaintance with some of the leading political figures there, helps me separate matters of moment far more easily than some other commentators. Yet, I realise that the culture in the academy is moving away from investing in long-term academic projects informed by a deep knowledge of a country's culture and history. The current fashion favours short-term, project-driven, outcome-oriented research. All this is necessary, I suppose, in these hard days of economic rationalism. But I hope that this will be a passing phase. There is no substitute for sustained, sensitive engagement.

A year later, Fiji's political problems remain unresolved. George Speight, incarcerated on Nukulau Island — once the quarantine station for Indian indentured immigrants — is still awaiting trial for treason, the case delayed ostensibly because the prosecuting authorities have been unable to find sufficient evidence to convict him of the high charge. A new Fijian political party comprising Speight supporters has named him its president, and wants his unconditional release so that he can stand for the general elections scheduled for August 2001. Others, speaking in the name of reconciliation, want the past forgiven altogether, the coup perpetrators pardoned. But genuine reconciliation will come only after the truth of what happened, and why, is fully understood by the people of Fiji so that history does not repeat itself.

The interim military-backed administration is engaged in a massive vote-buying spree among the Fijian voters, promulgating policies and programs which, it knows only so well, have failed in the past. The dream of indigenous Fijian political unity is as unrealistic now as it ever was. A new Fijian political party is born virtually every week, exacerbating the problem of fragmentation which had caused the downfall of Fijian-dominated governments in the past. Fijian leaders are embroiled in provincial and regional rivalries, bereft of a larger, overarching national vision for their people and for the country as a whole. They want power because 'it is their turn at the helm', not because they have a plan to take the country out of its present morass.

The Indo-Fijians are also divided over the means and methods of confronting the problems facing them. Their leases of native land are expiring, and they wonder whether these will be renewed, and on what terms. The sugar industry, which has sustained generations of Indo-Fijians, faces a bleak future in a globally competitive economy. Emotionally uprooted and made to feel unwanted, the best and the brightest are leaving for other shores, taking with them skills and experience the country can ill-afford to lose. Those who cannot leave hope that their children will. Meanwhile, the country is marooned in the shallows, divided and drifting. So much potential, so many missed opportunities. In the words of T.S. Elliot:

For our own past is covered by the currents of action,
But the torment of others remains an experience
Unqualified, unworn by subsequent attrition.
People change, and smile: but the agony abides.

The Dry Salvages

THE SUN SET AT NOON TODAY

Brij V. Lal

1. Fiji: The Gathering Storm

'Trust is like a mirror,' says Apisai Tora, Fijian nationalist leader from western Viti Levu. 'Once broken, it can't be restored.' It is arresting imagery, but coming from Tora, it sounds incongruous. Mr Tora is a veteran party-swapper, having been a member of virtually every political party in Fiji in a mercurial career spanning four decades. His latest handiwork is the spectacularly mis-named Party of National Unity, which fought the recent general election in coalition with Prime Minister Mahendra Chaudhry's Fiji Labour Party. Two of its four members in Parliament are in the current Cabinet. Mr Tora wants them out, and he wants Chaudhry to go as well. 'Indians came as slaves, and they are now our masters,' he told Radio New Zealand a few days ago. Fiji, he says, should have a Fijian Prime Minister. Nothing less will do.

Mr Tora lacks political credibility, but he is not the only Fijian leader attacking the Chaudhry government. Another is the opposition leader, Ratu Inoke Kubuabola, coup strategist, Taukei Movement stalwart, a reluctant supporter of the present Constitution, and currently the chair of the Cakaudrove Provincial Council. His province has passed a vote of no confidence in the government, and is likely to be followed by others in a carefully orchestrated campaign of anti-government propaganda among Fijians. Ratu Tevita Bolobolo, Tui Navitilevu, is the chair of a recently formed landowners council, Matabose ni Taukei ni Vanua, attacking the government and threatening the non-renewal of the expiring native leases to (mostly) Indo-Fijian farmers. Taniela Tabu, former Taukei Movement supporter and trade unionist with a chequered career, and head of the newly formed Viti National Union of Taukei Workers, is accusing the Chaudhry government of 'Indianising the public service'. The charge is baseless, but effective among Fijians already distrusting of the government. They are encouraged by the waning national influence of powerful chiefs like Ratu Sir Kamisese Mara, President of Fiji, and the absence from the centre stage of Sitiveni Rabuka and other leaders of moderating influence.

The government also has some silent foes within. Members of Labour's coalition partner, the Christian Democratic Alliance, labelled the government anti-Fijian over its hesitation to renew the work visa of expatriate Fiji TV head Kenneth Clark, because the Fijian provinces hold the majority shares in the company headed by Mr Clark. Poseci Bune, CDA's parliamentary leader and currently Minister of Agriculture, was talking of leading a coalition of Fijian parties against Chaudhry soon after getting elected, until he was inducted into the Cabinet. Members of the Fijian Association, another coalition partner, have similarly been critical. Deputy Prime Minister Adi Kuini Bavadra Speed, who is currently facing an internal revolt against her leadership, pleaded for the conversion of Chaudhry to Christianity.

A part of the reason for the orchestrated campaign is the politics of revenge. The former ruling party, the SVT, which now has only eight seats in the House of Representatives, will play rough and hard against those who caused its downfall, adopting expediently extremist positions, and injecting race into every issue of public policy to embarrass the government. A part of the difficulty for Chaudhry, too, arises from the manner in which his coalition won the election. The parties in the fractious 'People's Coalition' were united not so much by a common agenda for social and economic reform, but more by a desire to get rid of Rabuka and his government. Each wanted Rabuka out for reasons of its own: because of his government's sad, scandal-ridden record, because of the coups he staged (though not entirely by himself, Rabuka now concedes), and because he somehow sold out Fijian interests in the constitutional review process. But now that Rabuka is out of politics, the task of forging a common ground among the Coalition partners, with their own agendas and ambitions, is proving more difficult.

An important reason for Labour's victory in the May 1999 elections was its electorally appealing but generally uncosted program for social and economic reform. The party and its partners promised to reverse wholesale structural reform, strengthen the social safety net for the disadvantaged, and introduce a minimum weekly wage of $120, among other similar promises. The promises will take time to deliver, and there may be some need for re-adjustment and re-direction of public policy. The rhetoric of the hustings may have to re-adjust to the realities of governing. Understandable in rational terms, but a godsend to the racially motivated opposition parties bent on bringing the government down.

The Chaudhry Cabinet is new and inexperienced, learning the responsibilities and challenges of government as it goes along, on the job, with all the hiccups that the learning process involves. Its counterproductive tussle with the media could and probably should have been avoided. The issue of working visas for expatriates could have been handled more sensitively. Chaudhry himself, supple and resourceful, is learning to make, not without a hitch, the transition from trade union leader to national leader, just as Rabuka did a decade ago, moving from the military to the national stage.

The overwhelming sense in Fiji is that the mandate of the ballot box should be honoured, and that Chaudhry should be given time to prove his mettle. How long? That, of course, is the question. For people like Apisai Tora and others like him, the time is up. Meanwhile, there is no shortage of problems for the government to tackle. The resolution of the land lease problem, balancing the interests of the Fijian landowners and the largely Indo-Fijian tenants, is one. Reassuring a Fijian community bombarded by anti-government propaganda is another. To meet the challenges of the 21st century, Fiji needs to move gradually but decisively away from the futile politics of race toward a more inclusive non-racial culture of politics. Turning back the hands of the clock will not do the clock any good. Lessons of the past will have to be learnt anew. In the words of one sage, 'The best prophet of the future is the past'.

2. Damaged Democracy

Fiji is a damaged, divided democracy. George Speight's dramatic intervention has dislocated the process of political reconciliation, severely strained race relations, and shattered the foundations of the nation's economy just when Fiji was gradually emerging from the debris of 1987. The images of looting and burning, thuggery and violence on the streets of Suva, the worst in the history of Fiji, will forever remain deeply embedded in the collective consciousness of its people, and the recovery from the wreckage and ruin will be long and hard.

George Speight, a Fijian of Part-European descent, a failed businessman, an Australian permanent resident, proclaimed himself as a saviour of the Fijian 'race'. The Constitution, which only three years ago was unanimously approved by the Fiji Parliament (the majority of whose members were indigenous Fijians), blessed by the Great Council of Chiefs, and praised by the international community, had to go, he said. The government of Fiji must be returned to indigenous Fijian hands.

Speight is the frontman for a variety of interests, including the radical nationalist Fijians operating on the fringe of indigenous politics, opportunistic Fijian politicians defeated at the last elections keen to settle old scores, and an assortment of people from various social and ethnic backgrounds who rode the gravy train of the 1990s, but whose prospects dimmed upon the election of Mahendra Chaudhry's People's Coalition government. They were not pleased, and they threatened reprisal. Elements of the military, too, are involved, especially members of the crack Counter Revolutionary Warfare Unit established by Sitiveni Rabuka after the 1987 coups. Their involvement is the inevitable consequence of a politicised armed force whose loyalties lie with individual leaders than with the institution of the army

The Chaudhry government's hectic — in the view of some of his critics, too hectic — legislative program heightened their fears. The Prime Minister's pugnacious style, forged during his long years in the country's trade union movement and his government's ongoing, hugely counterproductive confrontation with Fiji's media, worsened the situation.

coup

The government was understandably pressed by its political opponents to deliver early on its electorally appealing but economically costly election promises, including introducing minimum wages, providing social security, rolling back the structural reform program, and resolving the ever-difficult issue of expiring leases. Land, always an emotional issue in Fijian politics, became the rallying point for Fijian groups already distrusting of the government and galvanised into action by the dormant Taukei Movement by that mercurial chameleon of Fiji politics, Apisai Tora whose own party is Chaudhry's coalition partner. Such is the nature of politics in Fiji.

The problem, if there is one, is not Mr Chaudhry's ideas and his vision for Fiji; it is more his style and the tradition of open, robust political discourse it represents which does not sit easily with the other tradition of more allusive and indirect discourse, conscious of well-defined cultural protocols, rank and hierarchy. Removing Chaudhry from power will not solve Fiji's ever-deepening social and economic problems in an increasingly globalised world. The land question will have to be resolved sooner rather than later because the Fijian sugar industry drives the engine of the national economy. The state, whoever runs it, cannot evade responsibility for the fate of people turfed out from the leases after generations of earning their livelihood from them, nor ignore the legitimate interests of Fijian landowners who want them back. The principles of good, effective and transparent governance will have to be observed irrespective of who is in power.

Speight and those who support him want a reversion to the 1990 Constitution which enshrined Fijian majority in Parliament and to the principles of ethnic dominance which underpinned it. But even with greater numbers, Fijians could govern only with the support of non-Fijian parties because they have splintered into political parties bitterly opposed to each other. Rabuka lost the 1999 election in large part because of Fijian political fragmentation. The same will happen again, for Fijians, like other communities in Fiji and elsewhere, are divided by ancient prejudices and modern greeds. And the fragmentation will increase with the gradual disappearance of the fear of Indian dominance which has informed political discourse in Fiji for the last half-century.

The culture of political patronage that emerged in the 1990s brought the country to the verge of bankruptcy, epitomised most notably in the near-collapse of the National Bank of Fiji. Well-connected opportunists had a field day. Virtually every public institution became infected by the virus of mismanagement or abuse of office. The most seriously affected victims of this were the ordinary Fijians of all ethnicities. But there were also some who benefited unscrupulously from the public coffers, and some of them are among the moving agents behind the present crisis. Returning to 1990, as Speight and his supporters demand, will once again hobble the institutions taking Fiji towards better governance.

Race has been portrayed in the media and popular commentary as the main issue behind the present turbulence. It is an issue, but there is more to the story than meets the eye. Speight has trained his sight on the Indians, but he is also leading a middle-class revolution against the Fijian establishment symbolised by Ratu Sir Kamisese Mara. The disrespectful and dismissive (once unthinkable) tone in which his name is being taken, the call for his resignation, the increasingly audible whispers about his supposed dynastic ambitions, the long reign of the eastern hierarchies of the Koro Sea, touch deeper issues about the structure of power in traditional Fijian society than is first apparent. Race becomes a tool for mobilising Fijian opinion, for in the ultimate analysis this crisis is more than about Indians.

Mahendra Chaudhry is not the problem facing Fiji today. You may remove him from power, but the deep-seated problems will not be removed. You may maim the messenger, but the message will not go away.

3. Wandering Between Two Worlds

The promises have gone
Gone, gone, and they were here just now

W.S. Merwin

The abrogation of Fiji's 1997 Constitution has saddened me immensely. Part of the reason is personal. As a member of the three-man Fiji

Constitution Review Commission, I had a small hand in devising it. Our report was a comprehensive document based upon the most extensive consultation in Fiji, a close first-hand examination of the constitutional arrangements of jurisdictions with problems somewhat similar to Fiji's, and expert advice drawn from the South Pacific region and international experts in Europe and North America.

The Constitution, based on our report, was unanimously approved by an ethnic-Fijian dominated Parliament and blessed by the Great Council of Chiefs. Now it lies tattered in the dustbin of Fijian history.

I feel deeply sorry for the ordinary people of Fiji of all ethnicities as well who will have to pick up the pieces from the wreckage of the last 12 days and start all over again. The task of reconstruction will not be easy. The fabric of multiculturalism and harmonious race relations has been severely strained. The philosophy of multi-ethnic cooperation on the basis of equal citizenship has been discarded. The economy, which was beginning to show signs of recovery after years of stagnation caused by mismanagement, and an insecure investor confidence, is hobbled. However you look at it, the hostage crisis is a huge disaster for Fiji. It has put the country back at least a couple of decades.

Fiji has failed the ultimate test of democracy: to survive a change of government. We now know what havoc a gang of armed thugs can wreak. George Speight, front man for an assortment of interests, has achieved virtually everything he wanted. The People's Coalition government headed by Mahendra Chaudhry is out of power. The President, Ratu Sir Kamisese Mara, has been forced, however gently, to vacate his office. The timing and the manner of his departure, under armed guard in the middle of the night, brings to an end an illustrious, though not unblemished, career. He was the last of the great chiefs who ruled Fiji. The multi-ethnic Constitution, prepared after such exhaustive consultation, is out. And Mr Speight and the seven men who hijacked Parliament and held the Prime Minister hostage, have received amnesty. Mr Speight, volatile, dangerously delusional, the self-appointed saviour of the indigenous Fijian 'race', even though he himself is half-indigenous, is savouring his gains and demanding a place at the head of the country's political table: he wants to be Prime Minister. If he has his way, there will be more Speights in Fiji in the future and, one fears, in other South Pacific states where the roots of the democratic tradition are dangerously shallow.

There are other casualties of this crisis as well. Among them is the Great Council of Chiefs. Formed by Sir Arthur Gordon soon after Fiji became a Crown colony in 1874, it occupied an honoured place in Fijian society as the government's and the Crown's principal adviser on indigenous affairs. Sadly, it stands today as a diminished body of dithering men and women, confused, partisan, manipulable, unable to exercise their much sought after — and much hoped for — role as the custodians not only of indigenous Fijian but also of Fiji's broad national interests. The chiefs have grievously breached the trust bestowed in them by the nation. They listened to Speight's pleas for Fijian paramountcy, but there was no place in their deliberations for the voice of a multi-ethnic democracy and the defence of a Constitution which they themselves had blessed just three years ago. They have showed themselves to be parochial men and women, bereft of a broader vis on, chiefs with a small 'c'. Unelected, unrepresentative and dominated by chiefs of the east, especially from Mr Speight's Kubuna confederacy, they will meet on Monday to decide the political future of Fiji: whether Fiji will continue under military rule, or whether it will be governed by a so-called civilian rule under the leadership of George Speight and his men. A wrong decision at a critical moment will spell doom for them. Already, western Fijians, long resentful of eastern hegemony and demanding greater recognition for the disproportionate contribution they make to the national economy, are gathering to decide whether they want to remain in their present position or seek a separate state for themselves. They have no problems with the Indians, they say, with whom they have lived side by side for well over a century. But their voice is under-represented in the Great Council of Chiefs.

Fiji's much praised military forces, too, have had their reputation tarnished. They vacillated while the country burned, terrorised into immobility by armed thugs roaming the streets of Suva. Why, it will be asked for some time yet, did they not intervene earlier, and more decisively, to prevent a catastrophe they knew well was coming. Allegations of complicity cannot be dismissed and, one hopes, would be investigated by an impartial body. Be that as it may, there is no doubt the Fijian army of today is not the army it was some years ago, an institution of integrity and professionalism. Now the military is deeply divided, its ranks infected by the deadly virus of provincialism. Had the crisis gone on longer and martial law not been imposed, thereby testing the regional and personal loyalties to chiefs and *vanua* (land, place of birth), it is not too far-fetched to say that the army would have fragmented into separate provincial militia. In view of its lacklustre performance in protecting the security of the state, and its blatantly partisan and racially exclusive character, the people of Fiji may well ask whether Fiji should have an army at all. If that is not countenanced, then it will be in the interests of the indigenous Fijian people themselves to have more and more non-Fijians enter its ranks to diffuse provincial tensions. Keeping the status quo is a recipe for disaster.

This crisis, everyone now knows, was more about the restructuring of power in indigenous Fijian society than it was about race. Knowledgeable commentators are saying that the support base for the coup is in the Kubuna confederacy from where all its leading thinkers and strategists come. They were ascendant in the 19th century, and they want to regain their place in the Fijian sun after a long period of wandering in the political wilderness. But the crisis is also in some sense about a cry of those Fijians marginalised by modernisation and globalisation, feeling left by the wayside while helplessly watching as others marched on to good and greater things for reasons they cannot comprehend. Speight's mesmeric rhetoric and simple solutions touched a chord with them. Get rid of the Indians and revert to Fijian tradition, and the world will be well. It is not as simple as all that, and Speight and his advisers know that only too well, but they cynically manipulated innocent and confused Fijian emotions for their own ends. The crisis was not about Fijian identity and tradition. In any case, identity is a process that changes with time, and there is no one single, cohesive Fijian identity and tradition to speak of except in opposition to other groups.

Indo-Fijians are the meat in the sandwich. They are trapped, terrorised into silence. They are still regarded as '*vulagi*', foreigners, in their own land of birth, where they have lived for four to five generations, descended mainly from the 60,000 indentured labourers brought to the British colony in the late 19th and early 20th centuries to work on Australian Colonial Sugar Refining Company's vast plantations. When their five years contract ended, most settled down to a life of agriculture. They have no land although they drive the engine of the country's agricultural economy. The thirty-year leases they occupy are expiring, with renewals looking remote or taking place at exorbitant rentals. And now, once again, they face the stark prospect of political disenfranchisement and unequal citizenship, and that, too, for one, and one reason only: because they are of a different ethnicity. Their plight deserves more sympathy than is usually shown in an age dominated by the rhetoric of indigenous nationalism. Unwanted and humiliated, many will understandably seek to re-build their lives in other countries, and one hopes that countries which have benefited from their labours, especially Australia, will show sympathy for a people condemned to a life of permanent servitude in their land of birth.

Meanwhile, Fiji drifts, divided and uncertain, into uncharted waters. An era has come to an end, and another is in the throes of a difficult birth. In the words of Matthew Arnold, Fiji is poised to

Wander between two worlds
One dead and the other powerless to be born.

AN HISTORIC VIEW OF FIJI

Hugh Laracy

Let me begin on a personal note. In mid-afternoon on 14 May 1987 I was hurrying along William Street in Sydney when I caught a glimpse of a newspaper billboard that I thought carried the words 'Coup' and 'Fiji'. Curious but not concerned, thinking that I had either misread the notice or that it meant something other than what a literal reading would suggest, I carried on to the news-stand on the next corner. There, the reading of a newspaper confirmed that what I thought — or merely hoped? — had not happened, had in fact happened.

The month-old, democratically elected government of Timoci Bavadra had in fact been overthrown by armed rebels. Despite being a professional student of Pacific affairs and a regular visitor to Fiji since 1966, I was surprised by this dramatic turn of events, not because it had been entirely unpredictable but because, on the contrary, it was the realisation of a possibility that, hoping against hope, one had long feared but had hoped but preferred not to contemplate. For there were long strands of communal division in Fiji's history that linked the present disquietingly to the past. Consequently, when on 19 May [2000] George Speight and a group of armed and masked myrmidons presumed to overthrow the constitutionally elected government by an act of terror putatively undertaken on behalf of the indigenous Fijian sector of the nation's population, the news came more as a disappointment than as a surprise. For not only are there structural fault lines that can be a source of tensions among Fiji's peoples, as shelves of books can testify, but those divisions are also susceptible to being distorted, magnified and perversely exploited by miscreants and the misguided, especially among the Fijians. George Speight is a case in point.

Ironically, the Indian community at which Speight's animosity is primarily directed has been the saviour of the Fijian people. Despite the prejudices of Speight's sympathisers, a group which extends well beyond its overt supporters, the Fijians' debt to the Indians is incalculable. They began incurring that debt in 1875, a year after Britain, accepting Ratu Cakobau's second offer of secession, agreed to annex Fiji as a colony. Returning from a visit to Sydney, Cakobau and his two sons brought measles back with them, and in the space of a few months over 30,000, a fifth of the population, died from the disease. When Arthur Gordon, the first resident governor, arrived in June 1875 to establish the colonial regime, he was therefore confronted with an ailing people; one which in its sad plight he likened to the Scottish peasantry of his day, with which he likewise sympathised.

Consequently Gordon, and his ally John Thurston, framed politics designed to preserve the Fijian population, to keep its society and traditional culture intact and to maintain their ownership of the bulk of the land. To this end, in order to provide the supply of cheap labour required to service the European-owned plantations, which supplied the revenues needed to sustain the government and its policies, he imported labourers from India. The first of them arrived on the *Leonidas* in 1879 and the last in 1911. By 1920, when the last of the labour contracts had expired, over 60,000 Indians had been brought to Fiji, and many of them had settled there. In the words of one historian, JD Legge, they represented 'a kind of human subsidy to Gordon's Fijian welfare policy'. Life on the plantations had not been easy for them, '*narak*' ('hell') they called it in Hindi, nor was it always much better after 1920. Still the Indians strove to improve their position through education, by going into business and by farming on their own account (usually on leasehold land).

An unyielding pattern had, however, been set. As early as 1875 Lord Salisbury, the Secretary of State for the Colonies, had decreed that any Indian settlers who had completed their labour contracts 'will be in all respects free men, with privileges no whit inferior to those of any other class of Her Majesty's subjects resident in the Colonies'. While Indians, then, might be entitled to — and expect — parity with other citizens, that entitlement was consistently limited in Fiji by the administration's adherence to the counter principle of maintaining 'the primacy of Fijian interests'. That is, Gordon's policy of providing privilege and protection for the indigenous people, the Taukei, prevailed. If in the game of the survival of the fittest the Indians often won it was always through their own efforts. In 1977, for instance, following a government decision to reserve 50 per cent of its scholarships to the University of the South Pacific for Fijian students, Indians needed 261 marks to win a scholarship whereas for Fijians the qualifying mark had to come down to 216 for their quota to be filled.

More directly relevant to the current messy situation has been the readiness of Fijians to find advantage in skewed constitutional arrangements. Led by Ratu Mara, the Fijian-based Alliance Party provided Fiji's first government on the attainment of independence in 1970. But Mara had only agreed to accept independence on condition that the constitution contained a gerrymander in favour of the Fijians. Even so, there were some among the Fijians who, aware of what Idi Amin had done in Uganda, had also hoped that independence might bring the expulsion of the Indians from Fiji. The strength of that sentiment, and its ability to embarrass the compromising Mara, was seen in the election of April 1977. The Fijian vote was split by the rise of the explicitly racist Fijian Nationalist Party led by Sakeasi Butadroka. Accordingly, the Alliance lost its majority in the Parliament, leaving the Indian-based National Federation Party as the largest group there — and hence the potential government. Four days later, though, when its leader Siddiq Koya went to Government House to be sworn in, the Governor-General informed him that he had already re-appointed Mara, to form a minority government. A new election in September returned Mara and the Alliance with a secure majority, but the events of April carried grave portents. They revealed the depth of anti-Indian feeling among some Fijians, the inclination of Mara that he was the natural leader of the nation and, possibly most reprehensibly, the neglect of the Fijian leadership to assure its following that an Indian-controlled government would not have the constitutional power to interfere with Fijians' land ownership or with their valued social and cultural institutions.

Given the lofty insouciance of the Alliance, little had changed by April 1987 when the Fijian vote again split, this time with many of the more urbanised, professionally trained and better educated Fijians making common cause with the self-reliant Indians. Thus, a Labour–Federation coalition government led by Dr Timoci Bavadra came to power, only to be met with protests from unruly mobs appropriating the name and status of *taukei*, and interpreting Mara's fa from power as a blow to their racial pride and to their presumption of untrammelled sovereignty. The agencies responsible for maintaining law and order in the society were unwilling to take firm action to suppress the *taukei*, so a month later the army under then Lieutenant Colonel Rabuka dismissed the elected government and established military rule. Within a few hours of the coup Mara, who appears to have been indifferent to the unruliness of the *taukei*, accepted an invitation to join Rabuka's Cabinet. In December, when Fiji declared itself a republic, Mara again accepted appointment as Prime Minister. These interim arrangements lasted until 1992. Then, following elections under a new Constitution that vitiated the Indian vote, a civilian government, but with Rabuka now as Prime Minister and Mara as President, came to power.

International pressure and also, it should be noted, reasoned voices within Fiji called, however, for the 1990 Constitution to be replaced with a more democratic one. That was duly enacted in 1999, and in the ensuing election Rabuka was defeated by his Indian rival Mahendra Chaudhry. But on 19 May 2000 after a year of efficient and honest, if at times brusque, administration Chaudhry's government was forcibly disrupted by Speight. This action can be interpreted in the light of Speight's personal agendas and those of various private interest groups, but its wider significance, and especially the responses to it within Fiji, are to be found in a fuller context.

Speight's attack on the Parliament fits into the pattern of the historical events just outlined in various ways. Most obviously, he is the latest exponent of the extreme anti-Indian position aired in the mid-1970s in the rhetoric of Fijian nationalism by Butadroka. Then, there is the assumption of a Fijian entitlement to paramountcy that has become embedded both in official policy and in common Fijian thought. Then there is the Vicar-of-Bray-like adaptability of Mara, ever ready to bend to the prevailing breeze, as long as it is Fijian. Then there is the army, from which Indians have long been excluded, and which in 1987 preferred to topple the government rather than risk shedding the blood of Fijian rioters, and which in 2000 could be expected to show similarly delicate and partisan sensibilities. Then there was the knowledge that with some unequivocally disloyal soldiers to help him carry out his hijack he could count on the sympathy of a cross-section of Fijian society extending from the *taukei* rabble in the streets to the Great Council of Chiefs. Considering such factors as these, it becomes clear that from the start Speight had a better than average chance that his gamble would succeed.

And such seems to have been the case. Four weeks after the hijack he has not yet released his hostages, and the authorities have still not taken decisive action against him. Mara has resigned after conceding Speight's demand for an amnesty and for the abrogation of the Constitution. Meanwhile, the rebel leader's supporters have burned and pillaged shops and houses, raped Indian women and destroyed Indian property; and have even murdered a policeman. Yet the Great Council of Chiefs is still not prepared to disown his enterprise; military personnel fraternise with him; and Speight himself is not afraid to venture outside the Parliament which he has occupied. All this is sadly predictable. Rabuka, the president of the Great Council, spoke for many — but not all — Fijians in saying that he sympathised with Speight but disagreed with his methods. In the circumstances, it was an egregiously mild rebuke. Indeed, it is not inconsistent with a measure of connivance, at least indirectly so, in Speight's adventure.

Speight claims, with dubious altruism, to have acted on behalf of and in the interests of the indigenous Fijians. Yet, despite the readiness of many of them to believe him, he has not only severely destabilised the economic system, the social structure and political order of Fiji, all of which were finely balanced. He has also challenged the political philosophy which underpinned the broadly comfortable conditions of life that prevailed there. By denouncing democracy as a foreign ideology, a sneer also commonly heard from indigenous nationalists elsewhere in the Pacific, and by elevating indigeneity to be the source of what amounts to a divine right to rule, he has activated other social faultlines besides the Fijian–Indian one.

Democracy is a system that enjoins respect for (or, at least, resignation to) such things as restraint, tolerance, inclusiveness, egalitarianism, acceptance of variety and co-existence with 'otherness'. Now, in his assault on this system, Speight has raised issues that a peaceful Fiji would be advised to be reticent about. These are such matters as the fissures between the western (Melanesianised) chieftainships and the eastern (Polynesianised) ones, those between urbanised and rural Fijians, those between chiefs and commoners, those between young and old, those between traditionalists and modernisers, and those between people who wish to see their lands profitably cultivated and others who merely wish to assert ownership of them. Talk of a western Fijian independence movement, reviving memories of the Western United Front of the early 1980s, is a symptom of these divisions. So, too, are the difficulties that have hindered the established authorities in coming to a consensus about how to handle Speight. And so, too, is Speight's ability to spend so long playing cat-and-mouse with them, while so many of his supporters seem determined to bring Fiji to a state of barbarism and for the farms to revert to bush.

If there is an argument about democracy in all this, it is not that Fiji is not ready for democracy, or is unsuited to it, but that it needs it in order to avoid the disruption that is likely to flow from any enshrinement of indigenous sovereignty. Those indigenous innocents from Fiji's Pacific neighbours, not least of these from New Zealand, who have endorsed Speight's claims out of sympathy for what they see as an indigenous cause, would be well advised to revise their opinions about what he has accomplished. For in attacking the Indians, whose habits of industry have contributed more than any other factor to the nation's commercial economy and to the growth of a local professional class, he is attacking people whose historic role in Fiji has been to benefit the Fijians — as Governor Gordon intended.

REFLECTIONS ON THE CIVILIAN COUP IN FIJI

Tevita Baleiwaqa

I stepped on to the Fenner Hall shuttle at 11:07 on the morning of 19 May 2000. I stopped short on the door when I heard the 11 o'clock Australian Broadcasting Corporation news, '...there is an unconfirmed report of a coup in Fiji!' But as the shuttle turned on to Northbourne Avenue, the newsreader confirmed that Mahendra Chaudhry and his Cabinet had been taken hostage. I was shocked but excited. This is a personal reflection on this crisis.

This paper reflects on the coup in Fiji. The coup itself was a strategic operation. The coup operation, from the drawing board to execution, can be detailed and presented as a discussion paper on the subject of toppling governments. But the subject of the coup, the Labour government of the Republic of Fiji, is pregnant with all categories of issues for discussion. Therefore in this reflection, I prefer to select current issues within the Fijian section of the population in Fiji, which directly forced this coup to take place. I do not intend to judge the coup as right and wrong, for what is done cannot be undone. Furthermore, there are many experiences which can be used as issues for reflection, like the hostages' experiences, yet I have chosen issues which are institutional rather than personal for my reflection. I will therefore reflect on momentary angst deduced from this crisis. Do not judge me as a presumptuous Stoic, for I am conscious of the twinge each individual citizen in Fiji is going through.

I called the General Secretary of the Methodist Church in Fiji, the Reverend Laisiasa Ratabacaca, and asked him of the Church's point of view regarding the coup. He gave me a rainbow answer, assuring me that this turmoil will soon be over for a new era of Fijian history to be born. I base my selection of issues on that eternal rainbow from Epworth House in Suva, and not on the temporal flood which overflowed only for 40 nights. The civilian coup in Fiji happened when I was working on the Reverand John Hunt and Joeli Nau's legends of the mythological civil war and the successive flood at Nakauvadra. It was an event whereby the chiefs of Fiji waged war with one another. The Nakauvadra flood did not have a rainbow in the sky, but the birth of chiefly titles from that flood to become the institution of hope for the Fijian society could be a good moral to the legend. I will not deviate into this subject for it is in my thesis. I prefer to refresh my mind with current issues engulfing Fiji before I return to Nakauvadra and complete my chapter on Fiji divinity.

I must briefly clarify the form of addressing chiefly names and Fijian traditional political boundaries in this article. I prefer to address Fijian chiefs by *Ratu* before their personal names, due to my respect for the families concerned. The chiefly families in Fiji are divided into three major confederacies. They are Kubuna, of which Bau is the head; Burebasaga, under the leadership of Rewa; and the Tovata, under the leadership of the Cakaudrove chiefs. These confederacies existed before the nineteenth century. Rewa, for instance, had been acknowledged as the political capital of southern Viti Levu and adjacent islands of Vatulele, Beqa and Kadavu. Bau later emerged as the political capital of the northern half of Viti Levu in the mid-nineteenth century. The amalgamation of the northern and eastern chiefs, to be called the Tovata, was the result of Ratu Goleanavanua and Enele Ma'afu'out'itonga's efforts to set up their own sovereign government. Even though these traditional political systems were established beyond the nineteenth century, the customs and laws are still enforced within the modern Fijian society. Within these three confederacies of Kubuna, Burebasaga and Tovata, there are fourteen provinces. In Kubuna, there is Tailevu, Naitasiri, Ra, Lomaiviti and parts of Ba. Burebasaga consists of the provinces of Rewa, Nadroga, Serua, Namosi, Kadavu and parts of Ba. The Tovata confederacy consisted of Cakaudrove, Bua, Macuata and Lau. The structure of the chiefly system varies from province to province. In Tailevu for instance, there exist three other divisions, namely Bau, Verata and Nakelo. Ra consisted of four chiefly districts, Saivou, Rakiraki, Nalawa and Nakorotubu. These confederacies and provinces formed the traditional basis of contemporary Fijian politics. Beneath the modern politics of the Fijian political party, the Soqosoqo ni Vakavulewa ni Taukei, there is an interflow of a strong combination of Fijian traditional and chiefly politics.

The issue of Fijian alarm at losing political control. Mahendra Chaudhry's Labour Party had overwhelmingly claimed victory in the May 1999 general election in Fiji. The ruling Fijian political party lost, with its coalition partner, the Indian-dominated National Federation Party. Before a year had gone while in office, the Labour government began to hear the voice of Fijian political discontent. It rather surprised me that the coup had to be staged so early, in relation to the three public protest marches. I had thought that the Fijian opposition to the Labour government in Fiji would continue to keep 'Mahen's nose to the ground' by public pressure. Hence my saying-so inclinations towards those protest marches in Suva. The mere fact of three public protest marches in three months should have given to any analyst indication of something of this calibre. The Police Commissioner, Colonel Isikia Savua, was not surprised. He was sharp enough to cage it, but the then Prime Minister Mahendra Chaudhry ignored his security assessment warnings.

The major element of my surprise was not Mahendra, but Ratu Sir Kamisese Tuimacilai Kapaiwai Mara, the Tui Nayau, and Ratu Josefa Iloilovatu, the Tui Vuda, as President and Vice President respectively. Ratu Iloilovatu himself is a *vasu* to Cakaudrove. In a coup situation, like in Fiji, where one replaces a government thought to be arrogant in one's own eyes, the Head of State remains unaffected. Unless you overthrow the Constitution, then the coup can affect the Head of State. What surprised me most, therefore, was the toppling of a government under the constitutional noses of two ranking Fijian chiefs. Once the executive government is sacked, how can these two chiefs and the Constitution function? It surprised me that sentiments had reached this extreme stage where the proletariat had undermined the aristocrat's constitutional footing.

I tried to regain my thoughts and tried to place myself in the mind of those who staged the coup. I did not know who they were really. There must have been a lot of recent political developments in Suva that I do not know, apart from those news flashes released through the two news web sites, Fijilive and Fiji Village. Even though surprised, I was thrilled also after hearing the news. It is now an exciting opportunity for thinkers to analyse latent social forces of Fijian societies that need only an event like this to reawaken them. This is another chance for the nation to examine its heart and other state vital organs; and especially to review the spirit of Fijian island political and social life.

The issue of racial politics. The conflicting political goals of the two major races in Fiji commanded Fiji's political scape. What are these *ends*? This is the question that animates my academic curiosity. Let me reflect on this question on a larger political scale in order to contextualise the coup d'état. The Fijian political goal is *total political* control over their islands. But to the Indo-Fijian population, it is *political power sharing*. The confrontation of the two *ends* caused the current crisis in Fiji. The two former Fijian Prime Ministers, Ratu Sir Kamisese Tuimacilai Kapaiwai Mara and Sitiveni Rabuka, tried their best to deal with these two ends but they were toppled through ballot by Fijians who did not want to share power with Indo-Fijians. When Mahendra Chaudhry, an Indo-Fijian Prime Minister, came into power, the Fijians toppled him by force, on the thought that the ballot paper was too late. They saw that it was not going to be *power sharing* but *power lost,* even though Mahendra's Cabinet had more Fijians than Indo-Fijians.

These conflicting political goals, in my view, cannot be related or resolved in Parliament. The concept of multiracialism, which had been Ratu Tuimacilai's dream, could have been settled first outside Parliament. In fact, in rural areas of Macuata and Ba, Fijians and Indians are bilingual. Bi-linguism is a good base for multiracialism. The problem then was how to translate the bilingualism of Ba and Macuata into a political reality. Parliamentary language is English but, under the skin, it is Fijians and Indians. The Fiji Parliament should be based on the answer to the two conflicting ends. It should not be the forum where we try to find the answer to the two political ends. The attempt to design a common future, identity and people in Fiji's multiracial mix failed when first George Speight and then Commodore Frank Bainimarama abrogated the 1997 Constitution. The failure of the 1997 Constitution does not mean the failure of racial harmony in Fiji. Fijians were not satisfied with how their political life was constituted in the 1997 Constitution. Hence their public protest.

The Fijians wanted to be respected in all levels of the government of their island state. I have therefore formed a term to identify what they want. Fiji is an *island state* with *island mentalities*. In this kind of mentality, boundary is an important issue. Boundary is a compound of political, religious, geographical and historical ideas. Boundaries are not only cartographic lines but also rivers, mountains, seashores, islets and reefs. It is an island because there is a sea around it. In this *island Christian context*, the Fijian view of humanity is an all-embracing totality. This totality is expressed in the concept *vanua*, connected yet unique. The norms of the *vanua* are expressed in Fijian natural hospitality — embracing, caring and loving, and with the widest smile in the world. He has his own set of customs and laws, which govern life and property. The British colonial administration, by regulation and ordinance, preserved most of these customs and laws.

The Fijians, I believe, do not intend to isolate the Indo-Fijian from this cosmological totality. And neither will they try to force a revocation of citizenship or deprival of Indians' voting rights. They do acknowledge their presence and contribution. But when it comes to political power, Fijians prefer all politicians to respect Fijian customs and laws, especially with recourse to the Great Council of Chiefs. All they want is respect of what is Fijian in a Christian and an island situation. *Viti is not only their land, but their islands as well.* This is all they have got. Both Viti Levu and Vanua Levu islands have been surveyed, claimed and registered. Fijian tribes own approximately 83 per cent of the Fijian landmass. Even the residence of the Head of State in Suva is on native land. The customs and laws, which governed these lands, are all according to Fijian customs. When the Labour government tried to play *free politics,* irrespective of customary laws and regulations and not considering the chiefly system, unconscious of traditional boundaries, taking advantage of the supremacy of the Constitution over Customary Laws, which govern land ownership, the

Fijians responded by public protests. Anglo-continental definition of democracy had to be redefined through island standards to give democracy its own unique island features. Fiji must be given the opportunity to redefine for itself this unique democratic mixture without outside interference. If it is not Fijian, it has no future in Fiji. If democracy is the *love of humanity*, then Fijians are prepared for it, in their own customs and traditions. But they will not forfeit their heritage in exchange for a democracy defined by another society. What Fiji is going through is a constitutional crisis. The world should allow Fiji to shape its own definition of democracy.

The issue of Fijian political leadership. This issue emerged when Fijians questioned Sitiveni Ligamamada Rabuka's morality. It was never an issue until 1987. After Independence, Fijians saw in front of them three prominent chiefs, Ratu George Kadavulevu Cakobau, the Vunivalu of Bau; Ratu Penaia Kanatabatu Ganilau, the Tui Cakau, and Ratu Tuimacilai. Their patriotism to these chiefs, especially to Ratu Kadavulevu and Ratu Penaia, were forged in battle and rugon by fields. Ratu Tuimacilai spent most of his time studying and returned to enter the colonial service. The Fijian soldiers who went on peace-keeping duties in the Middle East remember him for composing a song about them while they stood on duty. All three entered the Legislative Assembly and then into the Fiji Parliament, succeeding one another as Governor-General and President of the Republic of the Fiji Islands. I must say that the catchphrase in the current crisis, the end of the Mara dynasty, is a poignant axiom. The current dynasty, for me, is not a Mara dynasty, but the *Cakobau, Ganilau* and *Mara* dynasty. Ratu Sir Tuimacilai may be the last survivor, yet he is merely upholding their corporate legacy. As I compare how Ratu Sir Penaia handled the 1987 crisis and how Ratu Sir Tuimacilai handled this one, they have their own style of doing their duties. Ratu Sir Penaia was a man of the *vanua* and Ratu Sir Tuimacilai a man of letters. It is my zealous longing for the three families to come together and unite the fourteen provincial chiefly families so that Fijians may once more stand united. I do have a lot of faith in the new generations of chiefs, such as Adi Samanunu Talakuli Cakobau, Ratu Epeli Ganilau, Adi Koila Nailatikau, Ratu Filipe Tuisawau, Ratu Sakiusa Makutu and Ratu Inoke Kubuabola. The shadows of the former generation might be too huge for the latter generation, yet given the chance to lead, they will truly illustrate that they were born Fijian chiefs. The short period from 1987 to 2000 showed that the Fijians were receptive to the idea of persons other than those from their chiefly ranks to lead them politically. Their political loyalty will be offered if they see their chiefs uniting and leading them. The intricate network of Fijian tribalism which exists on village level summons these young chiefs to stand to their calling as Fijian chiefs. They were born to be Fijian chiefs.

As I write this short piece, the hostage crisis in Fiji has not been resolved. I wish I were in Suva to experience the anxiety, frustration and share in the hope of those who struggle otherwise for a happy Fiji. I found it hard to focus on my thesis, including a seminar on Fijian divinity. I am in the Coombs Building of the Australian National University, from where I am making these distant reflections, but my mind and heart are in Suva.

AN ANALYSIS OF THE CURRENT POLITICAL CRISIS IN FIJI

Teresia Teaiwa

The problem with Fijian nationalism is that there is no Fijian nation. There are Fijian provinces, and traditional Fijian confederacies, but the two military coups of 1987 and the current hostage crisis illustrate with disturbing insistence the erosion of indigenous Fijian social order and the fragmentation of indigenous Fijian leadership.

The problem with prevailing analyses of the political situation in Fiji is the notion that the conflict is between indigenous Fijians and Indo-Fijians. The 'race' card is misleading and mischievous, and unfortunately, Mahendra Chaudhry, Fiji's first Indo-Fijian Prime Minister, played right into it with his abrasive leadership style. But in the end, Chaudhry is not the problem and neither are the Indo-Fijian communities.

Fiji's problem is Fijian. Following the fortunes and misfortunes of the country's three indigenous Prime Ministers — Ratu Sir Kamisese Mara, Dr Timoci Bavadra, and Sitiveni Rabuka — we see the increasingly problematic configuration of indigenous leadership in the country.

Ratu Mara's leadership draws on the *mana* of his own chiefly title, Tui Nayau; his wife's *mana* (the Roko Tui Dreketi, from the confederacy of Burebasaga, is the highest chiefly title in the islands); and his close association with a tight elite cohort of European, part-European and Indo-Fijian business interests. Ratu Mara's leadership, however, has alienated rival chiefs, proletarian and nationalist groups within his domain of eastern Fiji, and has generated resentment in the western provinces.

The late Dr Timoci Bavadra, Prime Minister in the predominantly Indo-Fijian Labour/National Federation Party coalition government, was consistently described in the media and literature as a 'commoner' even though he came from a noble Fijian background in the chiefly village of Viseisei. The problem with Dr. Bavadra's political genealogy in 1987 was not so much his Labour ideology nor his 'commoner' status, but the fact that significant and powerful sectors of indigenous Fijian society — in the east — were not ready for a Fijian Prime Minister from a western province.

Being both a 'commoner' and national leader clearly was not a problem for Sitiveni Rabuka. In fact, a large part of Rabuka's popularity with indigenous Fijians is his 'commoner' status. For indigenous Fijians Rabuka's *mana* comes from the interweaving of his traditional '*bati*' or warrior genealogy (in the eastern province of Cakaudrove), his career in modern armed forces, his identification with and deployment of Christian/Methodist discourse, his staging of the two coups d'état in 1987, and the support he has consistently received from the Great Council of Chiefs. Rabuka has even gained political mileage out of his 'human frailties': sexual and financial indiscretions, as well as flip-flopping policy decisions which have increased rather than diminished his appeal.

Many indigenous Fijians identify with Rabuka much more easily than they can with the aristocratic Ratu Mara. Counterposed in this way against the elder statesman of Fiji, Rabuka developed his own ethos of popularism and 'can-do' capitalism — exemplified by the National Bank of Fiji debacle. During his Prime Ministership, a brash nouveau riche elite of 'indigenous' Fijians developed and thrived. George Speight is a good representative of this group, but an even better example is his mentor and benefactor Jim Ah Koy: both illustrate a new opportunism in regards to identity politics in Fiji.

A 'general elector' MP in the 1970s, Chinese-Fijian Ah Koy was sent to political coventry by Ratu Mara for insubordination. Concentrating his energies in business during the 1980s, Ah Koy's phenomenal success became worthy of a Horatio Alger story. In the first post-coup election of 1992, however, Ah Koy re-emerged as a political candidate, this time on the indigenous Fijian electoral roll. Although his eligibility to stand as a Fijian was challenged by other indigenous Fijians, Ah Koy won his case in court, and has represented his maternal constituency of Kadavu in Parliament ever since.

Like Ah Koy, George Speight's father, a 'part-European' and former general elector named Sam Speight, became a 'born-again Fijian' in the post-coup era. Sam Speight legally changed his name to Savenaca Tokainavo, winning an indigenous Fijian electoral seat in Parliament in the 1992 and subsequent elections.

In Fiji's disconcertingly racialised electoral system (comprising three electoral rolls — Fijian, Indian and General) general voters have historically aligned themselves with indigenous Fijian chiefly interests. The category of general voters covers Fiji's multitude of ethnic minority communities: Banabans, Chinese, Europeans, Gilbertese, 'part-Europeans', Samoans, Solomon Islanders, Tongans and Tuvaluans.

'Part-Europeans' form the largest and most influential group of general voters and in the post-coup era have shifted away from their historical identification with colonial European privilege towards a reclamation of their 'part-Fijian' or *vasu-i-taukei* roots. This shift in 'part-European' identification reflects a recognition of the contemporary realities of political power in Fiji: *indigenous Fijians rule.*

George Speight claims to represent indigenous Fijian interests. Sporting his European name, speaking exclusively in English, drawing on his Australian and American degrees in business for *mana*, and wearing his designer clothes, Speight does indeed represent indigenous Fijian interests. But Speight's indigenous Fijian interests are clearly neither the indigenous Fijian interests of Ratu Mara nor those of the late Dr Bavadra.

Speight's version of indigenous Fijian interests probably coincides in many areas with Rabuka's version of indigenous Fijian interests. But the men Speight has surrounded himself with also represent a changing of the guard from Rabuka's Queen Victoria School Old Boys network to an unlikely coalition of relatively young 'old boys' from Marist Brothers High School (Ratu Mara's alma mater) and Suva Grammar School.

And what of Speight et al's relationship with the marching/looting masses who were so inspired by the illegal actions in the House of Parliament on Friday 19 May 2000? It is a relationship of convenience:

Speight has about as much respect for the 1997 Constitution he once congratulated Professor Brij Lal on, as he does for the indigenous *marama* in *sulu* and *jaba* helping herself to bales of cloth through the shattered window of a Waimanu Road store.

The march was organised by church and Taukei Movement leaders, and though the looting may not have been planned, they certainly enabled it. Looting has become an ominous feature of recent indigenous Fijian responses to crisis: during the floods of 1998, at the tragic crash site of flight PC 121 in 1999, and now in the streets of Suva — 'the millennium city'. The image of a humble, God-fearing, dignified and hospitable people marketed by the Fiji Visitors Bureau is chillingly contraverted. The chiefs and church ministers stir their people but the simple truth is they do not control them: a group of alert and ambitious businessmen has used this feature of Fijian leadership to its advantage. Indigenous Fijians rule, but indigenous Fijians are not united.

This puts the past 12 months of the Mahendra Chaudhry Labour Coalition government's rule in perspective. The government has survived this long because of the backing of Ratu Mara. The government is in crisis right now because other indigenous Fijian groups are challenging Ratu Mara's authority. Rabuka has recently acknowledged this: the real struggle is amongst indigenous Fijians, and it is continually masked by the rhetoric of a racial conflict between indigenous Fijians and Indo-Fijians.

The impoverishment and disaffection of indigenous Fijians are not a result of 12 months of leadership by an Indo-Fijian. It is the result of 30 fraught years of modern indigenous Fijian leadership that have sacrificed the economic and cultural well-being of a people for the advancement of a few.

Speight's ignominious entry into the national and international limelight is but a symptom of the complex contradictions and competing interests facing indigenous Fijian society today. George Speight has not only kidnapped a democratically elected Prime Minister and his Cabinet; he has taken hostage much of the hope and potential Fiji had at the turn of the century to become a nation united. And when the present crisis at Fiji's House of Parliament in Nasese passes, as it inevitably will, the question will remain: what is Fijian nationalism when there is no nation?

CONSTITUTIONAL ORDER IN MULTI-ETHNIC SOCIETIES

Yash Ghai

One of the most interesting issues in constitutional theory today concerns the political organisation of multi-ethnic societies. A key question is the extent to which ethnic identity should be recognised in public as opposed to private life.

A major criticism directed at the liberal democratic is that, in its preoccupation with individual rights, it refuses to acknowledge ethnic differences. It is argued that under the cloak of individualism, the values and mores of the dominant community are imposed on minorities, whether of gender, religion or culture.

The response to this criticism in places like Bosnia, Kosovo, Estonia and Hungary is the constitutional recognition of cultural groups through separate representation in the legislature and the executive, and special cultural or educational institutions

Fiji's experience of recent weeks shows the difficulty of organising the system of government in multi-ethnic societies. As in other colonies, Britain ruled Fiji through a policy of dividing the people into ethnic groups.

The separation of races went beyond the political to embrace educational, health and even economic institutions. Most colonies repudiated this principle when they became independent, in the pursuit of national identity and unity.

Fiji, however, did not do so, in large part because by then Indo-Fijians outnumbered the indigenous Fijians and the latter were afraid that a common electoral roll based on universal franchise in a Westminster-type system would reduce them to the status of a political minority.

With the active encouragement of the British, the indigenous leaders chose a system of communal voting that would guarantee them a parliamentary majority. The 1970 independence Constitution did ensure uninterrupted political hegemony for 17 years. The hegemony was reinforced by a strong ideology of traditionalism and chiefly order, in which high chiefs occupied positions of great economic and social privilege, in the manner of feudal lords.

The ideology emphasised the unity of the indigenous community, and habits of obedience by the commoners to the chiefs. Britain had established institutions, including the Great Council of Chiefs, and an ethnic Fijian army, to reinforce this sense of oneness. The entrenchment of Fijian land rights and the inalienability of land to non-indigenous persons had the same effect.

All this was done to preserve the 'traditional' system in the face of rapid economic and social changes. It severely hampered the ability of indigenous people to enter the modern economy by discouraging the enterprise of commoners and by social rules which valued collective property above individual possessions.

The chiefs became a kind of rentier class, living on rents paid by Indo-Fijian farmers or foreign hoteliers to whom indigenous land was leased. It is not surprising that this system came under heavy stress as indigenous Fijians were drawn into the monetary economy, principally as workers. More importantly, commoners obtained access to education and became increasingly resentful of their inferior position in the traditional hierarchy.

The system would have collapsed a long time ago had it not been for the presence of Indo-Fijians, who were placed in the role of the 'other', presented by chiefs as threatening the integrity and hegemony of the indigenous people — a theme the British had astutely used in the colonial period to divide the two communities.

Nevertheless fissures within the indigenous community by the 1980s allowed a predominantly Indo-Fijian coalition with some Fijian support to win the general elections of 1987 and form the government, led by an indigenous Fijian Prime Minister.

This government was overthrown within a month by an army officer, a commoner, with the active connivance of high chiefs. The new administration introduced a Constitution in 1990 which attempted to ensure a permanent indigenous parliamentary majority by increasing the number of seats for indigenous people and reserving key state offices to indigenous persons. Many other privileges were established for them.

The theory behind this Constitution was that of political order through the hegemony of one group over others, just like the white supremacy espoused by the National Party in South Africa and the Jews in Israel in their dominance over Arabs.

The consequences of this Constitution were disastrous: rampant corruption, decline in economic growth, outflow of talent and capital, and a general sense of alienation. Divisions within the indigenous community sharpened as the Indo-Fijians were sidelined.

In the mid-1990s there was increasing realisation that Fiji's political stability and economic progress depended on a constitutional order that was fair to all its communities, protected everyone's human rights, and was based on a national consensus.

These attitudes facilitated a constitution oriented towards ethnic integration, through non-ethnic seats in addition to ethnic representation, an electoral system which placed a premium on appealing to voters of all communities, and a system of executive power sharing, rejecting the exclusiveness embedded in earlier Constitutions.

The early experience of the 1997 Constitution, which also provided extensive protection of individual and collective rights of indigenous people, was favourable. Ethnic tensions decreased, ethnic-based parties began to integrate or co-operate across old divides, and even the appointment of an Indo-Fijian Prime Minister, with a truly non-racial government, was accepted without much fuss.

Once again, certain elements within the indigenous Fijians, sidelined after the elections, embarked on a coup. But this time the real impulses were not the displacement of Indo-Fijians, but competition for power within indigenous communities. As that storm-trooper, George Speight, has gone about his business, divisions within the indigenous Fijians have surfaced for all the world to see.

It was clear in 1987 that the chiefs were being used in narrow partisan ways, to lend legitimacy to a usurpation of power. It was equally clear that in the long run this would politicise their role, drawn as they would be increasingly into intra-Fijian quarrels.

The logic of that development has been well exposed by Speight's opportunism combined with his cynicism. If he has managed to bring many indigenous people together in his anti-Indo-Fijian tirades, his constant refrain that the 'real enemy' are Indians highlights the fragility of his coalition.

He has pitted high chiefs against high chiefs, the Great Council of Chiefs against the ethnic Fijian army, one confederacy against another. He, a commoner, has torn to shreds the ideology of traditionalism — all in the name of communal unity and hegemony. One of the many lessons that one can draw from this saga is that the modern preoccupation with 'identity' and 'difference' as building blocks of political orders needs to be approached with caution.

It is grist to the mill of opportunists and hate-mongers (as if the former Yugoslavia had not already taught us that lesson).

It fragments communities and denies our common humanity. Instead we should pay more attention to the framework of human rights which remind us of our common predicament and promise.

THOUGHTS ON FIJI'S THIRD COUP D'ETAT

Mere Tuisalalo Samisoni

George Speight has the support of the *vanua* and therefore informally the Bose Levu Vakaturaga (BLV), who are the trustees of Indigenous Fijian traditions and culture. Make no mistake, the issue for this third coup d'état, as with the first two, is indigenous rights and self-determination. Despite the design of indigenous structures, institutions and legislation to achieve that objective, it remains an ivory tower ideal. The system was unable to process a culture of development in tandem with indigenous aspirations and dreams for a better quality of life, even though the leadership role was in place. Ratu Mara did not deliver. The problem is an indigenous one being manifested in the '*kudru ni vanua*', provincial wrangling and political uprising. The discontent emanates from unequal distribution of the benefits of development, the democratic process and leadership.

I am not surprised that the dissatisfaction culminated in the third coup d'etat on 19 May 2000. This time it happened during the march organised by the nationalist Tako Lavo Party. The march was attended by the main indigenous Fijian political parties, SVT, FAP, VLV, Taukei Movement and the Tako Lavo, that make up approximately 80 per cent of the primary indigenous Fijian voters. These parties for the first time united to participate in the march, representing approximately 158,000 primary indigenous Fijian voters in the country, to express their powerlessness in the Mahendra Chaudhry Indian-led Labour Coalition government. In the May 1999 general elections, 1.9 per cent of indigenous Fijian primary votes went to the Labour Party. The balance, minus those indigenous Fijians with some primary votes in the Labour Coalition (98.1%–18.1%), are now in revolt in the people's coup d'état.

coup

From a management point of view, the product/service and market mix does not fit that which needs strategic thinking and management. During the colonial era, the development model was one designed for the colonial economy where raw materials and surplus were exported through the big multinational corporations and the laws were codified to support those activities. The colonial powers' export and pricing policies basically meant unequal exchange that exploited us, leading to our current underdevelopment. Hence the process of alienation began 125 years ago, so that today the majority of the *vanua* feel powerless, helpless and hopeless, resorting to collective survival tactics.

In the 1970s, when the leadership was questioned on the change of legislation from ALTO (Agriculture and Landlord Tenancy Act) to ALTA (Agriculture and Landlord Tenants Ordinance) and its subsequent pricing based on subjective unimproved capital value of the land, Butadroka, the champion of indigenous rights and land issues, was sacked by Ratu Mara from the Alliance Party because he dared raise concerns over the negative dynamics that had surfaced, embarrassing and violating the Alliance Party policy and stand on multiracialism.

Fijian leadership after independence did nothing to address this unrest so that today the indigenous Fijians are still marginalised from the development process for the sake of multiracialism that acknowledges our common goals but not our differences in culture and status of development. These facts are endorsed by the 1970 and 1997 Constitutions where the old order of centralised and imposed decision making continue to be the norm. The decisions are not decentralised, democratic or participatory, even though the structures, the Native Land Trust Board (NLTB), Bose Levu Vakaturaga (BLV), Ministry of Fijian Affairs (MFA) and Fijian Affairs Board (FAB) are there to process information and feedback for desirable changes as required by the traditional and new social orders. While indigenous culture and social capital or *veivakaliuci* includes the process of consultation and consensus, the grassroots indigenous input was assumed by the leaders to have been acquired by structural and role presence, but in reality indigenous rights and interests were not processed and took second place to international and regional interests, power, self-interest and the elite status of the leader, Ratu Mara.

For example, take the 1990 Constitution. The Generals or Others, who make up about 5 per cent of the population or 38,750, with approximately 18,000 voters comprising *Vasus* or relatives with European mixed blood from the colonial era, and minority groups were over-represented in Parliament. They have four seats to represent approximately 18,000 voters when it should be a distribution of approximately one seat per 6000 voters or a maximum of three seats for them. Having one extra seat means fewer seats for our indigenous people and their rights, and therefore a skewed emphasis on western civilisation and modernisation further alienating our people and culture. The grassroots indigenous Fijians were never actively consulted for their input, interpretation, understanding, consensus and acceptance to collectively integrate our Fijian culture, traditions and language into the development process, connecting who we are in identity, spirit, satisfaction and self-worth. Fundamentally self-identity is based on our spiritual relationship with our land and when that has been undervalued at the economic, social and political levels, that in itself begins psychological and ethnic cleansing, impacting negatively on our mental and emotional health, integrity, personality and social relationships. Loss of identity and dignity leads to social disintegration, which explains why indigenous Fijians, in 1998, make up 80 per cent of the population in prison compared to 51 per cent racial distribution in the general population.

In the meantime the trend of under-valuing and pricing continued in the leasing of our land under ALTA. So it is little wonder that after 125 years of contact with the outside world and because of core differences in culture with Indo-Fijians, our cultural strengths have also been marginalised from the development process, because our leaders have lost sight of their vision and role, abandoning us like lost sheep. When the migrant races want to dominate us economically and now politically, through the 1997 Constitution, even though we have a higher population distribution of 51 per cent, the so-called democratic system does not stack up for our rights and differences. The indigenous Fijians are overwhelmed by their lack of guidance to change from a subsistence to a cash, industrial, market and information economy in spite of all the money and scholarships given through the Fijian Affairs Board (FAB) to help us change and take responsibility for our output.

For the 1997 Constitution, regardless of the fact that the BLV rejected it by eight out of fourteen provinces, the central powers decided to push it through. For the sweeping changes it was expected to bring, such a document and subject should have been discussed at grassroots level, with input from our indigenous Fijian intellectuals at the University of the South Pacific (USP), followed by voting at a national referendum. This, regretably, did not take place.

The third coup d'état, with violence, burning, rioting, shooting and killing, and the experience in negotiations and mediation between the coup makers, the BLV, the President and the army are symptomatic of lack of *veivakaliuci*, the traditional democratic process taking place, which would have prevented these events. Instead, this time around, the situation disintegrated further into Fijian against Fijian and a leadership struggle for stewardship. The responsibility must rest on Ratu Mara's shoulders, as he was the leader unable to read the 'writing on the wall' and guide Rabuka. Their relationship grew into a battle of personalities when the young leader showed promise, culminating in the sale of his book on experiences during the army's first and second coups d'état which unfortunately did not deliver either. This conflict led to Rabuka trying to make a mark for himself in pushing for a Constitution that was way ahead of our time and inappropriate to our indigenous needs.

All these events lead us to believe that eventually the indigenous Fijian race and culture would be wiped out by a process of assimilation with the more advanced Indo-Fijian and Vasu communities in the economy, taking over with their western values, cultures and lifestyles. This is the reason for the *vanua* and indigenous support for George Speight. They have a cause to fight for. The third coup d'état is a grassé roots people's coup which removed their leaders Ratu Mara and the SVT Prime Minister of the previous government, Chairman of the BLV or mediator, Sitiveni Rabuka, because they did not produce for the *vanua*. Leaders by definition should innovate, bring about major change, and inspire followers to pursue extraordinary levels of effort. Ratu Mara and Sitiveni Rabuka should have addressed symptoms of underdevelopment of our people, through transformational leadership, using *veivakaliuci*, or consultation and consensus allowing the traditional democratic process to take its course. That participation would have empowered our people to take responsibility in the 'Amendments and modifications to the 1997 Constitution' paving the way to a 'home-grown model of development'. This course of action would have been more productive and meaningful. Taking the best from both worlds, western civilisation and our unique social capital, value systems, culture and traditions, relevant to the modern information and market economy, would guarantee the sustainability of not only our indigenous communities but others as well. This is a political reality because indigenous Fijians have always 'cared and shared'.

The negotiations and mediation undertaken at present without Ratu Mara, and Sitiveni Rabuka, but between RMF, George Speight and his team of advisers and the *vanua*, are at a very sensitive stage for an agreement on a line-up of advisers. Their terms of reference are to rewrite the Constitution while managing the country to return to normal operations and democratic rule. This will require a multi-pronged approach for law and order, building confidence in the business community and healing. What we do not need now is a group of senior job-seeking army officers, an 'army culture' of autocratic bureaucrats and centralised decision makers who by that very culture will kill initiatives to help us evolve out of this crisis. What we do need, however, are talented, creative and enterprising civilians and professionals who are committed to save indigenous Fijian culture and the motherland.

A.D. Patel and Jai Ram Reddy understood our differences, problems and common goals. Mr Reddy even offered to be the Deputy Prime Minister if the SVT/NFP/UGP Coalition succeeded in the May 1999 general elections based on multiracialism espoused in the 1997 Constitution. These were rejected outright by the Indian voters and Mahendra Chaudhry's Labour campaign message led to their overwhelming victory and majority.

The problem here was the new alternative and preferential system of voting. In the seat for Lami Open, which I contested, in some instances one vote had up to 10 values and others just one value. This is manipulated democracy. Democracy is one man one vote. What was wrong with the old system of first past the post, which is used in most developed countries? Even our social capital of *veivakaliuci* is more democratic than the manipulated hence flawed preferential system, to reach 50 per cent +1 to be elected.

Because of lack of time, we did not study the system to ensure the indigenous Fijians understood it for our preferences to win seats for our indigenous cause. But we were politically naive and ignorant. Perhaps we needed to experience failure to learn a very bitter lesson on vision and strategic management. The resulting dominance of the Indo-Fijian community in the last elections plus Mahendra Chaudhry's autocratic leadership style and interests threatened our very survival and the indigenous national extremists instinctively reacted, leading to the present crises. The signs were obvious but Mahendra and his indigenous Fijian Ministers were lulled into a false sense of security with their overwhelming majority, arrived at by a system of voting that was confusing, undemocratic and unwieldy. The system was amenable to corruption, buying preferential votes and party collusion. Voters did not understand it, which led to 15.9 per cent of invalid votes cast.

In summary, the colonial government left us a legacy where the social structures were changed from extended family and small groups to large groups and provincialism that protected colonial interests. The leadership and elite were rewarded accordingly, at the expense of the indigenous community, leaving a problem that is 125 years old. Another migrant race, the Indo-Fijian community, now wants to step into colonial shoes to control Indigenous Fijian development. The role of indigenous leaders has not been able to process change as desired by the *vanua* regardless of the structures, legislation and policies in place. This basically means ineffective leadership. The position has been vacated by Ratu Mara and Sitiveni Rabuka. The *vanua* is now crying out for a leader who will embrace our development philosophy of self-determination under ILO Convention 169. But he or she must be able to turn the belief into a way of life that governs mainstream behaviour and policy. Other races who support this belief need not fear for their security and safety as we wish to preserve our culture, tradition, language, a population of only 400,000 in the whole wide world and our motherland. Who will begrudge us this unique position?

The problems of leadership, development, democracy and our basic core differences with the Indo-Fijian community must be addressed once and for all, as no one agrees with the coup d'état method and its negative impact on cost, trust, goodwill and international relations. While it is justified to prevent indigenous Fijian community and culture from being wiped off this earth, there are also many Indo-Fijians who are happy to go about their lives and not politically dominate us. We do not want a nation tarnished with a coup d'état image. Instead (how the world should be through) we want a true democracy through parliamentary seat allocation according to population distribution, not by an imposed Constitution.

For the future, there are many opportunities that exist in the market economy for a 'home-grown development model' particularly at the macro level for indigenous rights and the micro level for small business development. Successful indigenous entrepreneurs are increasing due to the Affirmative Action Policy of the SVT government based on the 1990 Constitution. They can act as role models to guide indigenous people and enterprise culture while linking local villages to the global markets accessed by information technology and internet services.

At the core of any indigenous community is the need for sustainable development, that is environmentally safe, resource efficient, energy clean and financially viable. Subsequently, an appropriate and innovative option for government is to play an active role to promote green products and markets. Indeed that will facilitate productive and efficient processes and systems that are traditionally and democratically appropriate and dynamic. As such, our vision can only be bright for indigenous Fijian generations to come and those other races who believe in our survival.

The structure that has been changed and lengthened by the colonial powers 125 years ago must now be reversed and shortened to its original length. This will integrate the *veivakaliuci* process and improve the communication flow. Had the political will been active and indigenous grassroots and human input been systemised in the development paradigm, that feedback process could have avoided the three coups d'état and their debilitating national cost and wastage.

Sociologically, anthropologically, economically and politically decentralised stewardship and small group dynamics are the humane and strategic answer to our development problems. What is in dire need is a bottom-up empowerment perspective. Through empowerment-orientated organisation-building, people rediscover indigenous wisdom, recognise their potential and worth, learn new management and technical skills, reap due fruits of their development efforts, gain staying power, learn to demand what is due to them and at the same time become responsible citizens.

ON BEING FIJIAN

Taina Woodward

A speech presented to a conference of women at the United Nations, New York, 8 June 2000.

By now most of you have heard of the coup in Fiji. About 30 of our people are being held hostage. The President has been forced to resign and the Constitution put in place in 1997 has been revoked. The army has taken over and for the most part law and order have been restored. Most of the world thinks that little is being done to resolve the crisis. They are wrong.

I have been invited to this meeting as a Fijian, a housewife, and mother of three. In addition, with my husband I look after my mother and a nephew. I was born and raised in Fiji, I am a Fiji citizen, and I intend to die and be buried in Fiji.

I do not represent any government or organisation. I speak only as a Fijian, which in Fiji is understood to mean 'indigenous Fijian'. Other ethnic groups are called 'Fiji citizens', but not 'Fijians'. When I say 'Fijian' in what follows, I mean 'indigenous Fijian'.

I want to speak to you from the bottom of my heart and try to explain certain things about the Fijian values, customs, ways of communicating, mode of leadership, and sensitivities. I want to speak to you about the soul of Fijians. I hope that I can touch the souls of indigenous people everywhere.

We are a people who have occupied what is now the Fiji Islands for thousands of years. When we came, as far as anyone knows, no one else occupied the land. Our traditional oral history tells how we came and how we settled. Fiji is our 'Promised Land', the land of our forefathers. Our language and customs are at one with our people and our land and our genealogy.

In 1874 our land was 'ceded to Great Britain' under Queen Victoria. We were under attack by our neighbours, the 'Friendly' Islands of Tonga. In addition, our dominant Chief Cakobau was being blackmailed by the local American Consul and had no means of paying the extortionate payment demanded by this man for having accidentally burnt his own house down during a drunken Fourth of July celebration. American warships were on the way. Queen Victoria rescued us from these situations at the invitation of our paramount chief and we 'voluntarily', if you can call it that, became a colony under a Deed of Cession.

There were certain understandings at the time of Cession to Great Britain and there were many things left unsaid. One was that we would continue to be led by our own chiefs with our own style of government, a style that is called 'consensus'. But Queen Victoria also became our Queen. Another understanding was that while others were allowed to use our land, there was no such thing as the permanent alienation of our land, called 'sale' in English. In times of war, some chiefs sold islands out from under their people, but the intent here was to destroy or enslave the people, to detach them from their roots and their livelihood, to publicly humiliate them. If there is a meaning, this is the meaning of 'sale of land' in Fiji. Land is a sensitive issue in Fiji.

In fact there is no word in the Fijian language to describe the 'sale' of land, as the Western world knows it. It is not even a concept. If you were to sell your land, you at the same time sell your forefathers. The term 'sale' is sometimes used, but it really means 'lease', 'rent', or 'use' of land. This concept is familiar to many indigenous societies around the world, and it has been a source of great misunderstanding for people from around the world who have sought to acquire and settle land, and agony for those who thought it was perpetually theirs. We let people use our land and were surprised when they built fences and chased us away with weapons.

The British sent an expert to assess the economic potential of Fiji. This was around the time of the American Civil War and cotton was in great demand, so cotton was grown for a time. Later it was discovered that sugarcane was a more economic crop. Sugar became our major industry.

The sugar industry, like the cotton industry, required labour. We Fijians were self-sufficient nutritionally and economically with our abundance of sea and land resources. We were not interested in plantation labour. The British brought many workers from another of their colonies, India, to fill this need. These people worked hard, multiplied, and were allowed by the British Colonial Government to stay in Fiji.

At the time our chiefs ceded Fiji to Great Britain, we understood that other people would come and use our abundant land, but we did not foresee an open immigration policy or massive immigration. We did not know that we would come to be outnumbered in Our Sacred Homeland by people from another culture, many of whom did not wish to join our family culturally.

We Fijians pride ourselves on our friendliness and hospitality. We welcome visitors and we try to make them feel at home. We invite them into our homes. But we do not expect them to take over our homes, even if they arrive in great numbers. This has confused people from other cultures who do not understand Fijians.

Fijians live in a communal lifestyle, which survives by sharing. We give and we receive. When the missionaries came and told us it was more blessed to give than to receive, this was nothing new to us. Most Fijians adopted Christianity readily. We found the values consistent with our own. Fijians are very generous people, but within our own system, there are also obligations. Some people from other cultures do not understand this. They think that when someone gives you something, it is a 'good deal', a 'bargain', and you should take more, and more, and more.

The British brought non-indigenous people to Fiji for their colonial economic purposes. They came in great numbers. They were of a different culture with different customs from our own; they married young and multiplied rapidly. For the most part they rigidly clung to their native cultures, religions and value systems. Only a few joined ours. When the British left us independent in 1970, they also left us with a majority non-indigenous, not very well-integrated population. The British did this in a smaller way all over the world. Perhaps they did not see the problems it would create. Perhaps they did and slyly washed their hands of it. In some cases in Africa, people and their descendants uprooted by the colonial government were offered citizenship in Britain. So many wanted to go to Britain that they had to create two classes of citizenship. Not everyone who became a British citizen in the colonies was then entitled to settle in Britain.

Now Fijians welcome all kinds of people into their families. We especially like people who learn our language and customs. We have many instances of intermarriage and there are no taboos in this regard. But like all human beings, we tend to like people who like us. If people do not respect us, do not learn our customs, do not learn our language, do not learn to pronounce the names of places in Fiji correctly, after multiple generations living in Fiji, we tend to be suspicious of them. We especially don't like it if we perceive that such people try to take over our land and our government, and use fast economic growth, foreign aid, their concept of 'democracy', and 'strictly legal' means to justify it. This is not our way.

We do not like confrontation. When our people disagree, they remain silent. As you can well imagine, this is often misinterpreted by people who demand or expect that we tell them to their faces what we do not want. We want them to be sensitive enough to 'feel' that we don't agree. This is part of our culture.

Economically, Fijians like to do things in their own good time. This is not always fast enough for other people. We have no objection if they move quickly or move on as long as they do not 'step on'.

Politically, we like to make sure everyone agrees before we move forward. We don't like to dominate minorities with majority rule. We like people to feel good about any decision. We are a small place, everybody knows most everybody, and people who try to push their own way get nowhere in the long run. Our value system has much to offer the world. We intend to preserve it and offer it to others. But we are only 350,000 people in a very large world. Size does not bother us. Our rugby teams are among the best in the world and beat countries 500 times our size. We are known as peacekeepers with UNIFIL. The world needs to learn more harmonious ways of living and we have some good tips. But harmony usually requires the setting of and understanding boundaries of all kinds. We have our limits.

The current situation in Fiji is complex. There are many forces at work. The outside world sees primarily a racial issue. Fijians know that there is also a reconfiguration of power amongst the Fijians. There is a struggle between traditional Fijian confederacies, there is a call for a new confederacy, there is a struggle between the new middle class and the older traditions, and we women have also recently come into the political limelight. Reconfiguration of the Fijians is definitely our problem and no one else's. We will deal with it in our own good time. We welcome your views and un-tied assistance, but we will deal with it.

It is our relationship with our non-indigenous population that has attracted the interest of the world. The world media loves to talk about, exaggerate and exacerbate the problems of 'race'. It provides prime-time coverage and makes people not directly involved feel superior, no matter what they have inside them.

For more than 100 years, Fijians have lived side by side with our non-indigenous neighbours. We did not invite them, but we nevertheless welcomed them. We help them. they help us. We sometimes go to their houses and they often come to ours. We respect each other. We work together. We often drink and eat together. But for the most part, our cultures, and to a large extent our values, remain distinct. We believe that the vast majority of this population just wants to live and work peacefully in Fiji. We welcome this. We even allow them to get rich in Fiji, when few of us Fijians, because of our communal sharing oriented society, can ever aspire to this. Many of them, when they can afford it or have the opportunity, move on to more developed countries with greater opportunities. Some choose to stay and live in harmony with us.

But we have our limits. We have our land, our people, our leaders, our customs, and our souls. We want to be led by our own people who understand us and respect our customs. We cannot alienate any of our land any more than we can alienate our forefathers. Whatever the economic situation, the political situation, there is a boundary behind which we must fight for our survival as a people. No economic threats, bribery, media hype, or international organisation will step across this line. Some people call this 'indigenous rights'. It is the 'right to survive', have self-determination and ownership of our resources as an indigenous people in our homeland. This is in spite of TV, soap operas, The Simpsons, X-Files, global immigration and trade, all of which we enjoy in moderation just like you.

Recently, perhaps though the influence of TV, broader and better education, and general awareness, our people have become more vocal, and some even more belligerent. The emergence of previously quiet unspoken, usually smiling Fijians in our land is not unlike the emergence of women worldwide. We were not quite like this at the time Great Britain left us with a legacy of parliamentary government and a multiracial population. We listened to our chiefs and our chiefs listened to the Queen of England.

The recent coup in Fiji was conducted at gunpoint by a handful of Fijians and their spokesman, George Speight. Some guns were fired; these people shot no one, although they did put a hole in the roof of our new Parliament building. They took some 40 parliamentarians hostage and some 10 have been released because they were either ill, or willing to sign away their positions in the former government. One was allowed to go home to her mother's funeral, and then return. Even in crisis, we practise the Fijian way.

The verbal manifesto of these rebels included revocation of the 1997 Constitution, resignation of the President, and installation of their own group of people to run the government.

Some self-appointed 'supporters' of the coup went on the rampage burning, smashing, and looting the capital city of Suva. Some even stooped to racial violence, which was totally unnecessary and uncalled for. This is what happens when things get out of control. Every society has its hooligans with a grudge against the world. Our police were caught by surprise. Fortunately, there was surprisingly little violence. A few days later, the first real casualty was a policeman whose car was shot at by some of the rebel supporters when he ventured into an insecure area. Our ordinary policemen do not, and never have, carried guns.

Why then, didn't the police and/or the army march in and stop this? Why do the Fijians allow a small band of armed rebels to take over their government? Why did security limit itself to restoring law and order in the streets and not the Parliament?

The answer is simple. While most people were disgusted with the violence, the causes espoused by the rebels had a considerable amount of mass support, some of which was out in the open — thousands of people marched; some of which was implicit — refusal to act against the rebels. Strong feelings of resentment have been suppressed by Fijians for decades. To this day, the degree of support for the rebel cause is unknown because no one on the outside really knows what lies at the bottom of the heart and soul of every Fijian. The police force was divided on the basic issues as was the army. One can assume that the whole of the Fijian population is divided or uncertain on the issues involved. We need time to self-examine, time to discuss, time to let our traditional leaders know in our traditional way. The answer is not obvious.

Fortunately, outside nations did not step in. They are watching anxiously, but they are waiting to see if Fijians can solve their own problems. This is good. Bloodshed has been largely avoided, even while the threat and potential exist. Fijians need to be left to solve their considerable problems in their own way and on their own schedule. It takes time to reach a consensus. Interference can make matters much worse and not solve the underlying problem.

The news media are impatient. Every Fijian knows that the whole of Fiji is a hive of talk and activity. Formal and informal meetings are being held. The pubs are alive. The village kava bowls are flowing. The telephones domestically and internationally are abuzz. Gradually the chiefs will learn how their people really feel on the main issues. This is not a time for telling people what they want to hear, spouting religious moralisms, or pushing conventional wisdom. This is a time for searching out one's deepest beliefs and communicating them. Are we going to allow ourselves to be absorbed into the mediocrity of the modern world, or be dominated politically and economically by a foreign culture numbering nearly one billion people worldwide, or are we going to remain self-reliant and proud of our own culture of some 350,000 people? Are we going to claim our 'indigenous rights', or are we going to join the soap operas of the world?

There are numerous examples of indigenous peoples who have either disappeared from the face of the earth or have been marginalised in their own land. We can look around the Pacific Rim at New Zealand, Australia, the United States, and Canada, at countries where the indigenous people are found mainly on welfare rolls and in the prisons. They are an 'endangered species'. Why? Because they had different customs and traditions that did not stand up well to the onslaught and pace of colonialism and capitalism. Their souls were broken by their captors. They were, and still are, human, not material oriented, communalistic, but slower and less acquisitive. They had no powerful weapons. In addition, open or selective migration was promoted by the ruling cultures, so that the majority rule of democracy finished off the political marginalisation process.

This will not happen to Fijians. We are drawing the line. Some are openly fighting for our beliefs. We do not know yet how many will join in non-violent support. We will wait and see because we do not want a bloodbath and we trust our people and our traditional leaders.

What about our adopted non-indigenous brothers and sisters? They are part of Fiji. They have helped us as they helped themselves over the years and we sincerely hope they will continue to do so. We are basically a very peaceful and hospitable people. We espouse Christian values and we respect all religions. But we have learned the hard way that there is such a thing as giving away too much. We will not give away our sovereignty, our nation, or our souls. We will not allow our culture to be dismissed, absorbed or outpaced. We will do things in our own way and in ways we choose to adopt, because these are the ways we know best and the way we will not be tricked into something we don't want. We reserve the right to bicker amongst ourselves and move slowly without fear of being taken over by a united non-indigenous majority. This has been a problem with our electoral system. This is why many feel that we need a Constitution that while offering everyone some participation, guarantees us our land, our leaders and our ability to live and operate within our own cultural modalities. Such a Constitution would have to recognise and protect, in perception as well as in legalese, the indigenous rights of Fijians. We will have affirmative action in our Constitution, not in our welfare roles.

I repeat, we welcome and sympathise with our non-indigenous neighbours. We invite and want them to stay, in spite of the current turmoil. They are our friends and they have contributed much to the development of Fiji. They contribute in a major way to our economy. But they must accept our inalienable ground rules. Our own people will lead our own country as long as we have people to lead. And we will not divide our country. We are a difficult people to understand and especially to lead because our customs and traditions are different, and we tend to protect them. We would not wish this difficult task on anyone who is not fully accepted by our people.

As always, we want people who respect our culture, traditions, and language to join us and remain with us. We welcome everyone to our house, but please don't get the idea you own or should be the head of our house. As long as everyone understands these fundamental ground rules, Fijians will be at peace and continue to help bring peace to the rest of the world.

In Fiji we still believe very much in family values and we have roles for all ages, genders and relationships. While we have only recently risen to political prominence, political participation and women chiefs and other leaders have always been with us. There is more work to do. At this critical time, let me just say that I am moved by my heart to join my Fijian brothers, uncles and fathers in support, no matter which side they are on, as we go through this identity crisis as a culture and a nation. Fiji is all we have and we will keep it and maintain our God-given right to share it with whomever we want to when we decide to, without pressure from anyone.

We will protect and share our culture with you. We have our roots and our ancestral homeland. You are all invited to come to Fiji and share our hospitality and friendship. We will welcome you into our homes, our hearts and our hotels. This is part of being Fijian. We are proud of it and we will cherish and protect it always.

9

OUTCASTS
OF THE PACIFIC

Usha Sundar Harris

On Friday 19 May, Fiji once again felt the cruel hand of racism grip the island nation as it laboured to build fragile structures of social cohesion. Once again there have been calls in the streets of Suva to 'send the Indians back home'. As the hooligan element rioted in the streets, looting shops and burning property, the spirit of Indo-Fijians was broken again. Their home, their businesses, their very being felt threatened.

To them, this was another betrayal in a long line of betrayals through a history which saw the British colonisers bring Indians to Fiji as labourers, then abandon them without proper provision for land ownership or political inclusion.

Coup leader George Speight has told the world his actions are designed to protect indigenous Fijian interests against the ambitious Indians. We may as well be watching the events of 1987 when then coup leader Sitiveni Rabuka gave similar reasons for his actions after the Indian-dominated Labour Party came into power.

The news of this third coup in 12 years fills me with an overwhelming sorrow. The coups have forced many fourth- and fifth-generation Indo-Fijians like myself, who have never been to India, nor feel any kinship with that country, to look at our roots in an effort to understand why the Indian presence is so resented in Fiji.

How did we become the outcasts of the Pacific? Where do we belong?

The words of Indo-Fijian poet Dr Sudesh Mishra come to mind: 'The system, as it has been passed through the British and now taken over by

coup

56

the elite Fijians, has never actually allowed us to say that this particular grain of soil is yours, that you belong to it, that you can actually plant roots. So there is a kind of airiness between the earth and the feet for the Indo-Fijian.'

The feeling that Indians are the outsiders has been etched in the psyche of many indigenous Fijians through the nation's political processes and social structures.

I grew up in a racially mixed neighbourhood in the town of Nausori, 14 kilometres from Suva. During the festive seasons we shared foods and gifts with our Fijian neighbours or taught them how to make roti.

I was confronted by my 'otherness' one warm Sunday afternoon as I worked in the garden with my mother. A Fijian girl who had recently moved into the neighbourhood approached us and pointing to our house told my mother, 'Hey, kai India [Indian], one day I will live in that house'.

My mother was enraged by this affront. As an eight year old, I hoped that we would not have to leave because I liked my home, a rambling old bungalow which once housed expatriate managers working for the Colonial Sugar Refining Company (CSR).

After the 1987 coups, I began to read the history of Indians in Fiji. Slowly bits of information that had filtered in while listening as a child to my father's conversations became insights into a bigger picture.

The threat of the Indians undermining Fijian interests has been used throughout the colonial period to keep a check on Indian aspirations and to gain support of Fijian chiefs. The most anti-Indian ideas and attitudes in Fiji came from the Europeans. Whenever there was a need to control either Indian labour or Indian demands for political representation, the Europeans would bring up the greater right of Fijians.

The colonial government encouraged racially segregated schools, and prohibited Fijians from going near Indian settlements, prompting the two groups to see each other through a prism of prejudice and stereotype.

The practice of appealing to one race against the other to win votes later became the mainstay of political campaigning. When Rabuka seized power in 1987, the first thing he did was to separate the Fijian Ministers from their Indian colleagues. Speight has repeated this formula.

Neither Fijians nor Indians had any say in the matter of bringing Indian labour to Fiji. Britain ruled both countries. Fiji's first governor, Sir Arthur Gordon, saw it as a necessary condition of preserving Fijian interests. Indians would wear the responsibility of farming and labouring in Fiji, and thus save the Fijian race from colonial exploitation and even extinction. Between 1879 and 1916, more than 60,000 Indians were brought to Fiji as indentured labourers. With every 100 men came 40 women. a disproportion which would become the cause of major social upheaval in the plantation lines.

Among those thousands of souls separated from their homeland and loved ones were my great-grandparents. Enticed by promises of good pay and easy work to a land of plenty, instead they arrived in a land of fierce warriors, relentless hard labour and unrelenting sahibs, many of whom spoke with their whips and their boots.

Here their future became inextricably tied to the profits of white planters and to a powerful Australian company, CSR, an entity as powerful as the government of the colony. The Indians had a deep distrust of CSR and regarded it as the tyrant against whom they were to wage many battles.

After the Indians served their five-year labour they could pay their own passage back to India or stay in Fiji, or they could serve another five years and get a free passage back home. Many could not endure another five years of hard labour nor had the money to pay for their passage so chose to stay. Others had become estranged from their families in India and were forging new friendships in Fiji which had now become home.

As descendants of these labourers, Indians have continued to farm the same land over three or four generations leased from the indigenous Fijians, who own more than 90 per cent of the land in Fiji. Indians make up 43 per cent of the population but own less that 2 per cent of the land.

Despite the sacrifices of our forefathers, new generations of Indo-Fijians realise with sorrow that we may never be allowed to adopt Fiji as our own. The national memory of Fiji has a convenient amnesia when it comes to Indian history and the community's contribution to the nation's development.

So what becomes of a people who are treated as resident aliens in their own homeland? How do we cope with this instability?

When people are denied the privilege of calling their homeland 'home', denied roots, then they begin to look outwards to other possible landscapes where they can actually plant roots. Thousands of Indo-Fijians have migrated to Australia, New Zealand, Canada and the United States, a mass exodus taking place after the 1987 coup. No doubt another one will follow the present coup.

Like those Indo-Fijians, I also left Fiji about 20 years ago in pursuit of education. Ironically, I have kept my Fijian citizenship through the turbulent times in Fiji's politics, always hopeful that one day I may return home. But that is beginning to look highly unlikely.

It is easy to see why Fijians are endearing to Westerners. They are animated, they smile and laugh more easily. The Indians seem more withdrawn, inhibited, and don't smile as easily. The strangeness of two such vastly different cultures living in one land is painfully plain to a visitor. We are two very different people.

Yet, I believe that it is the common people in Fiji, both Indians and Fijians, who have contained an eruption of bloodshed in the streets after the coups, not the police or the army. Despite the resentment, there remains a basic decency and goodwill amongst the people in Fiji towards each other.

I have often pondered about the place called home. Home is not a place where we can be arbitrarily told to belong or not belong. Home is that favourite tree in the schoolyard, or that bend in the river, or that lonely hill beyond — places of our childhood deeply etched in the memory. Chiefs and coup leaders in Fiji may tell the world Indians don't belong in Fiji, but we know that Fiji belongs to us.

10

RACE, SPEIGHT AND THE CRISIS IN FIJI

Vijay Mishra

Race and ethnicity are not identical. In Fiji one suspects no one really cares about this crucial distinction. On 14 May 1987, Rabuka's rhetoric was racial; since 19 May 2000 George Speight's has been even more so. I begin my story with race because my Fiji was primarily colonial and racial. By the time I left Fiji for good in 1974 I had seen only a year and a half of post-colonial Fiji. By the flukes of colonial educational system and scholarship grants I had been in New Zealand and Australia between the mid-sixties and early seventies. Fiji called itself multiracial, never multicultural because it always emphasised atavistic allegiances to primordial difference, not differences that are culturally or socially constructed, as differences based on ethnicity always are. So while Anglo-American anthropologists (among them Australasians) in our part of the world began to redefine the study of cultures, the colonial administration in Fiji clung on to race as an immutable and genetic category. In the end that legacy made it impossible for ethnicity in Fiji to be theorised in anything other than racial terms by the native informants themselves.

As far back as I can recall race was how I was officially categorised although in actual practice, in terms of inter-communal relations, I don't recall ever being rejected by a Fijian on grounds of race. Racial division didn't mean much as we could communicate with Fijians in their native tongue. My father spoke impeccable Fijian and my grandmother — fondly called Adi Kelera by the villagers of Nakelo — spoke it as her native language. To this day when Fijians ask me *'o vaka tikotiko mai vei'* ('where are you from?') I reply, as Fijians always do, with reference to the village or province of my grandparents, in this case the depressed village of Nakelo. Other Indo-Fijians also do this, except those who have lived for generations in urban areas, but even there I can't think of any Indian who would not have connections through their cane-cutter grandparents to a village. Not that Indians actually lived in Fijian villages, their bastis or gaons simply took on the name of the adjoining village or administrative unit: Yaralevu, Vatualevu, Saweni and so on. But in spite of the symbiosis, the fudging of the absolute categories of race in favour of constructed ethnicities, the official line affirmed divisions in terms of race.

At Lelean Memorial School, the predominantly Fijian Methodist School that I attended, the small minority of Indians were there as representatives of the Indian race, presumably to give Fijians a bit of competition (which never happened because the Fijian students at Lelean were often brighter than us). At Suva Grammar School Indians and Fijians could study for their University Entrance Examination in a class that was called 'multiracial sixth form' because the school was exclusively for people who were Europeans or, like George Speight, part-Europeans or *kailomas*. Times changed, the British left, a post-colonial world order was established but race remained a formidable category and ethnicity undertheorised. In all this, of course, the kailoma (literally I suspect meaning children of love, but I am no expert on Fijian etymology) remained ambivalent. At Suva Grammar School they were despised by the Europeans. I recall the Headmaster, Mr Webb, saying to me in his office after he had taken the rather unusual step of naming me a prefect, 'don't be intimidated by the part-Europeans, they are not your equal'. He was alluding to the discipline problems they posed, as I soon found out during lunch-hour detentions. But I had no cause for worry with them. It was the Europeans who never took any directive from me, and simply ignored me throughout my two years at Suva Grammar School.

As for the *kailomas* many were from the sugar mills and were closely associated with the CSR and sugar plantation life because their parents were mill supervisors, engineers and so on. Their surnames were predictable — Williams, Heritage, Lobendahn, Bower, Simpson, Valentine, beachcomber names all. They were good curry eaters, some spoke in Fiji

Hindi (like Billy Heritage and Keith Williams from Nausori) and basically thought of themselves as a separate race. If they had full-blooded Fijian mothers they never spoke about them. As a group their silence was essential because their colonial privileges were based on their silence. And they did very well. They were the middle-level bureaucrats, sugar mill and copra workers, and many were planters in their own right. In the communal constituencies of the colonial government they were classified as Europeans. The Fijians, of course, had no vote until 1963 when between three to five (I forget the exact number) of Fijians could be directly elected to the Legislative Council. Before then all Fijian political representation was through nominations by the Governor and the Council of Chiefs. The Indians had had their communal constituencies for some time, going back to the late 1930s I think.

I thought of the *kailomas* in particular when I heard about George Speight, a name that I initially confused with Spate, author I believe of some important colonial white papers. To understand him is to understand the predicament of the *kailoma* in search of a racial niche denied him by colonial history. George Speight's plight is the plight of the liminal subject (curiously celebrated in postcolonial theory for his hybrid nous) who wants to move to the centre. In this move there is no redefinition of ethnicity (as one would have otherwise expected) but a reaffirmation of the colonial, absolutist category of race. Sitiveni Rabuka used racial discourse, Speight uses racist discourse, and there's the big difference. Colonial discourse was racial, Speight's postcolonial discourses (for he sees his coup as the extension of the uncompleted anti-colonial project of May 1987) are racist. The post-colonial — the post pax Britannica, those nostalgic years of peace — is now linked to the language of racial cleansing (not available when Marxist class analysis was still a valuable alternative to racial categorisation) and the coup seen as the final anti-colonial struggle, albeit against people who have been systematically dispossessed, deterritorialised and for a while after 14 May 1987 effectively disenfranchised. For the *kailoma* to ingratiate themselves into the *taukei* (the indigenous Fijian, literally the *bhumiputra*, sons of the soil), there has to be excess. Where there are colonial racial division, there has to be racism, where there is casual clothes of all variety, there has to be a return to the symbolic *sulu* (the Fijian Scottish kilt), where there is urban gait, there has to be village swagger, where there is at least token Indian representation, there can be none (no Indian names are mentioned in the proposed 'civilian' military council either). Speight's father changed his *kailoma* name to a dinky-di *taukei*, as did his mentor Jim Ah Koy. Behind the *kailoma* excess — his establishment taukei supporters would have found hostage-taking abhorrent — lies *kailoma* legitimisation. And because in the end, Speight has no village base as such (his life has been urban Fijian and Australian–American), his supporters are really the urban hooligans, the large sea of Raiwaqa (a Suva suburb) unemployed, the vulgar lumpen-proletariat who work at the behest of the reactionary Kubuna Fijian constituency who feel that the Mara-Lauans (with a dash of Polynesian blood) have usurped the power of the traditional chiefs (Melanesians) who ceded Fiji to Britain in 1874. The demands he has continued to make, demands almost invariably structured in the language of a student in a small-time undergraduate American university (Andrews in Michigan, I believe), are absurd in both substance and form. In spite of at times vicious communal rivalry among the Fijians themselves (as we have seen) in Fijian culture, you don't demand that a high chief (like Ratu Mara, the Tui Nayau, ex-President of Fiji) be unceremoniously removed. You take a *tabua* (a whale's tooth) to him and in the middle voice of formal Fijian ask his permission to replace him. It may mean the same thing, but the demand is enacted through a ritual that neutralises antagonistic dialogue. The urban *goondas* of Suva no longer understand the old decorum, as Speight himself, so characteristically, doesn't.

If I were a V.S. Naipaul I would have done my research and written a shorter version of 'Michael X and the Black Power Killings in Trinidad'. Research into the life of Speight — his formative years, I believe 12 in all, in the US and Australia, his failed business dealings, his hubris, perhaps even his pamphleteering and student politics — would have given us an insight into his sick megalomaniac mind. The crusader has no one but himself to advance, which is why the hostage crisis is so surreal, like a scene from the theatre of the absurd. Speight just doesn't make sense, but he gets whatever he wants. To put it another way, Speight makes sense only because he is a *kailoma*. In the end it is his failure to self-reflect upon his own history that will be his downfall. The excessive demands, the projection of an absurd heroism, his failure to observe *taukei* decorum, *taukei* control, will lead to an even further mockery of the kailoma by the Fijian. In bringing shame (*vaka-madua-taka*) to the very people he proclaims to represent, George Speight may bring upon the *kailoma* the very derisory stereotype he applied to the Indo-Fijian.

PEACE IN FIJI

John D. Kelly and Martha Kaplan

Much about ethnic Fijian culture is truly wonderful. But one of Fiji's most precious cultural resources is in grave danger. And this precious cultural resource is not part of ethnic Fijian culture. It is not *kava* circles, nor *mataqalis* and generalised reciprocity, nor *tabua* and the dignity of ritual hierarchy. This most precious cultural resource is non-violence, and while it has strong roots in the *loloma* (kindly love) that is the *mana* of Jehovah in Fiji, its widest and deepest roots in Fiji are Gandhian, and its most profound expression is now and long has been the forbearance and tolerance of the Indo-Fijians.

There are people in Fiji for whom *mana e dina*, 'mana is the truth'. What they see, and what they demand respect for, is the glory of power and status. And there are people in Fiji who seek and respect a truth whose highest realisations lie not in *shakti*, 'power', but in *shanti*, peace. There are lots of people in between, many respecting both forms of truth and some, neither. And these peoples cross-cut Fiji's ethnicities; one can find people whose lives are filled with love for a god of peace in any of Fiji's churches and in all of its seminaries, as readily as one can find them in the mosques, *gurudwaras* and temples, right down to the most remote of Ramayan *mandalis* or Sathya Sai centres.

The Gandhian tradition, that has done so much for Fiji, is rooted in religious love of god, peace and truth but it is also more than that. It brings a non-violent commitment to the truth into the heart of political processes like no other tradition of political ends and means. *Satyagraha* is the Sanskrit word Gandhi coined to name his political approach. Gandhi liked to translate it into English more than one way, sometimes as 'soul force', sometimes as 'insistence on the truth'. But a more literal Sanskrit translation is 'grasping the truth', 'holding on to the truth'. In Gandhi's hand the Christian and British tactics of righteous boycott and protest marches became dynamic vehicles of *swaraj*, 'self rule', as colonised Indians literally freed themselves from domination first of all by self-transformation, by realising their power to control their own expressions of consent and resistance. In Gandhian politics, the conscious *satyagrahin*, holding onto the truth, refusing to affirm untruth, chooses deliberately when and why to compromise and where and how to oppose the greatest threats and evils, especially when to sacrifice, not in anger but in duty.

It is not nearly well enough understood in Fiji, especially by outsiders to Indo-Fijian tradition, how many times Gandhian-inspired boycott, especially Indo-Fijian boycotts, have changed Fiji's history for the better, and shaped much of what is best about the Fiji of today. Long before the barristers sent by Gandhi, S.B. Patel and A.D. Patel, began their careers of good works in the islands, the Gandhian Bashisht Muni led the boycott in 1921 that clarified, once and for all, that the sugar industry could not continue on the basis of plantation-style labour contracts; CSR and government committed themselves to their experiments in Indo-Fijian small farming, much to Fiji's benefit as both profits and living standards were raised. The boycott of the Legislative Council and call for 'common roll' voting, begun in 1929 by the Fiji Indian National Congress, led by Vishnu Deo, was doomed in an empire whose racism was steadily increasing, but uncompromisingly raised the question of when and how Fiji could reach past the barriers of race, a question many in Fiji still need to face up to. And the cane boycotts of the 1930s and 1940s — yes, we would argue absolutely, even the bitter boycott of 1943, deliberately provoked and prolonged by a British governor reckless in his hatred of A.D. Patel and Swami Rudrananda — not only led Fiji to greater justice in industrial relations, but also (and even though so many have painted them matters of race and loyalty to nation) continued the process of finding, in economic truths, the way out of Fiji's heritage of colonial race difference and antagonism. All cane growers get the same price; garment workers' and other workers' wages respond far less to race than to markets, and the whole nation is hurt when government planning and contracting are corrupt.

You don't need us to tell you who George Speight is, what damage has been done to Fiji's economy and democracy by the cascade of terrible events that have followed on his rank and ugly opportunism. You don't need us to tell you how tragic is the decision of Bainimarama and the military to take it upon themselves to write a new Constitution. But there is something that perhaps we can observe, thinking comparatively and anthropologically about the Indian diaspora and the global politics of the last century. You probably already know that Fiji's 1997 Constitution was a progressive mix of globally informed multicultural democratic vision and locally attuned, pragmatic compromise. You may hope, as we do, that sooner or later, in one form or another, Fiji will see not merely its return but the arrival of a Constitution that better enshrines its guiding principles. But there is more to fear than its loss in the meantime.

While Suva is enveloped in a cacophony of discord, with ominous streaks and smears of disorderly violence, another cane boycott has far more quietly and non-violently begun in the west and north. As usual, the threats have come from the men of *mana*, not from the people wronged, not from those who voted for the cherished People's Coalition government now destroyed and held hostage, not from the people whose situation is now so precarious on the lands where they have lived their lives. What comes from them is not a threat, but a reality of non-cooperation. The army, now, won't allow meetings. It won't allow the boycott to have its leaders even to state its terms. Thus the truth this boycott insists upon remains inchoate, spontaneous and intense. Together with international economic boycotts it mounts an economic pressure, too, that is intense. But we promised a comparative perspective. And it is ominous.

Fiji is not only a nation that should take pride in the great gifts it has gained from its Gandhian heritage. It is also one of the last outposts of Gandhian-inspired political action where there is still a general public committed to a politics of non-violent boycott in response to injustice. It might be *the* last outpost, where Gandhian protests have not been answered by organised violence. Just about everywhere else with a Gandhian history, of whatever form of cultural transmission, from our own USA's civil rights movements to India itself, non-violent self-sacrificers have been overcome, at times, by the ruthlessness and contempt of their foes. To suffer non-violently, insisting on the truth is pointless, if the truth is that you have enemies who do not care about your suffering.

Ethnic Fijian leaders in quest of greater *mana* may decide, this year, to seek it by coercing or dispossessing their non-violent neighbours. There is even talk from some quarters of using the army to cut the cane and break the cane harvest boycott, something that has never happened before in Fiji. Or the suffering of the farmers may simply be ignored. In the long run, however, Fiji's current leaders may discover that their *mana* was actually underwritten in part by the forbearance of the lovers of *shanti*. If the current military government violently destroys a tradition of peaceful protest that has helped make Fiji great, or if they allow acts of violence to go unpunished, they will lose far more of their own world than they could have imagined possible.

We hope for a peaceful solution. In fact, we can envision the process, as in 1987 to 1997, leading to more perfect union, and possibly on a much shorter clock, given the skepticism about this coup in the outside world. But we are also aware of other possibilities, and fear for what Fiji is already losing, not least with every new passport issued: not ethnic Fijian culture, which has never really been threatened, but Indo-Fijian faith in a politics of peace and truth for Fiji.

ON RECONCILIATION

Christine Weir

Tonight, I am haunted by an image from the evening news. In a theological college, surrounded by garden, with a circular chapel as its centrepiece, military men and armed terrorists meet to decide the fate of a nation and probably to tear up its constitution. The press swarm around, and on the roadside youths with stones taunt passing cars. The staff and student houses on the campus are empty, vulnerable; among them are the homes of my friends. Fifteen years ago I taught English here to the students' wives, and it is a place of happy memories.

I had been forewarned. Internet and phone calls had informed me that the Fiji Council of Churches had been asked to provide a neutral meeting place for negotiations between the newly declared military government and Speight's men who have been holding the Fiji Cabinet hostage for 12 days. They offered the Pacific Theological College premises, just next door to the parliamentary compound. It is an old and honourable role for the church to provide a safe place, where people may attempt to be reconciled. The Lutheran church in East Germany provided such a place for meetings between civil rights activists and the Communist Party for years before the fall of the Berlin Wall. The offer of the Fiji churches falls within that tradition, yet I am still shocked by the image. It seems sacrilegious.

The chapel at PTC, its focal point, is dedicated to the memory of the islander missionaries, the covenant makers, those who travelled from their island homes across the Pacific to bring the Christian gospel to other islanders. It is dedicated to, amongst others, Tongan Joeli Bulu, who fought his mythic shark in the Rewa River, to Aminio Baledrokadroka, who pleaded with the colonial governor of Fiji to be allowed to evangelise in

New Britain, to Semesi Nau and Pologa, who sat for three months in a boat in the lagoon at Ontong Java before consent was given for their landing. It is a memorial to thousands of men and women who were prepared to give their lives — and many did just that. Some would say that they were the dupes of colonialism, forced to work for a pittance in areas deemed too dangerous for a white missionary. There is some truth in the charge. I have read the arguments over pay, the scathing comments made by white missionaries about the perceived shortcomings of their islander colleagues. Yet they were not forced, nor are they seen as duped. Rather they are seen by their descendants and by others as epitomising that which is best and noblest among Pacific people. It is here that the armed men come.

The image remains with me as I attend an ecumenical reconciliation service for Corroboree 2000. Tonight, for most of the congregation, reconciliation is exclusively about black/white relations in Australia, about indigenous rights here. For me, it has become more complicated. Can there be any equivalence between the struggle for the rights of the minority, the genuinely dispossessed in a settler society, and the manipulation of 'indigenous rights' by a majority to justify the dispossession of others? There are strident voices on the internet which would seek to persuade me that the two are the same. But I cannot agree. What links my walk on Sunday across Commonwealth Bridge in the sleet and wind, and the walk I will do tomorrow with the Fiji community is a belief that it is possible for different communities to live together in harmony, but only if the past is acknowledged, if there is mutual respect, if there is justice and equity. Three years ago I thought I had seen that belief in Fiji. Visiting for the first time in 12 years, I had watched services and ceremonies of reconciliation as the new, fair constitution was accepted. Now all that was blown to the winds. Had it been a chimera?

After the Corroboree service I describe the scene at PTC to a theologically inclined friend, and ask him whether he thinks the use of such sacred space for the negotiations is part of the church's role of reconciliation, or a sacrilege. 'Perhaps,' he replies, 'that depends on what they decide.'

TWO COUNTRIES CALLED FIJI

Bruce Connew

My two elder daughters both have Fijian partners. I hadn't thought this so extraordinary — until the coup. Then I began to think, how do I deal with this? One is an Indo-Fijian who arrived in New Zealand with his parents after the last coup, and the other an indigenous Fijian here on a university scholarship. They are almost as dear to me as my daughters. They get on well, and in fact once lived not far from each other in a middle-class suburb of Suva. But when we sat around the table talking after Speight had stormed Parliament, it brought to mind other conversations we'd had. I can remember thinking during some of those conversations that each of them was describing a different Fiji, a different country almost.

A week after Speight sets free the last of the hostages, I will watch my second daughter's Fijian partner caress her temple as a contraction takes hold. Before morning, they will have had a son, my first grandchild, a boy, the first boy of the eldest son, a half-caste, 'the boss', says his Fijian grandfather. The next day, the Indian partner of my eldest daughter will sit on the edge of the hospital bed, and hold the swaddled baby close to him as he reads the front page of a newspaper.

I'm keen to look around these countries, I tell them. My plan is to be back in plenty of time for the birth. Two days in Fiji, and the parents of my second daughter's partner invite me to a funeral. A big funeral. A paramount chief. Bau Island, powerful well beyond its few indigenous hectares. They lend me a school history book, so I'll better understand the weighty significance of Bau. It is day 39 of the coup. They tell me to

coup

photograph the ironies at the funeral, and I wonder how do you photograph ironies, and which are the ironies?

The coffin is all over the place, anything but level, as the pallbearers negotiate the mud of the steep and slippery slope to the tomb. I can see their shoulders reddening beneath the weight. Hundreds of mourners follow. What must be going through the minds of the dead chief's brother, Ratu Epeli Nailatikau, in his white shirt, tie and *sulu*, mud slushing over his leather boat shoes? The rebels have just released his wife. She is a daughter of Ratu Sir Kamisese Mara, the dislodged President, and is here today. In a few days, we will learn that Epeli is to be Deputy Prime Minister in the military's interim government. And after that, a Cabinet Minister in the post-coup interim government.

The first king of Fiji was from here: Ratu Seru Cakobau. He ceded Fiji to Queen Victoria in 1874. I smile, wondering whether Queen Elizabeth knew, on a visit to Bau in 1982, as she passed the spirit temple, handbag and white gloves, that beneath its four corners are the skeletons of four strong men, who, not all that long ago, were ritually buried alive with each corner post?

There has been no king of Fiji for the past 10 years, not since the last one died. The contenders among the Bau Island kingly families cannot agree on which of them it should be. Ratu Epeli is one of the five contenders. He says later in a newspaper story, his very thin upper lip prominent in the photograph, that this procrastination, the power struggle for the title, is behind the current strife. A rudderless Kubuna confederacy. And this is where the ironies begin to come in. There are three confederacies, and right now there is a clash between two of them: Kubuna and Tovata. The king, when there is one, is the traditional head of Kubuna. The most often seen leader of Tovata is Ratu Mara. Since independence in 1970, it has been Ratu Mara (and therefore Tovata) who has held most sway. Kubuna is reasserting itself.

The mourners at this funeral, I have drummed into me, *are* the ironies. I flick back to the names given to me the previous evening: tribal enemies, family enemies, political enemies, business enemies, and some of them all of these at the same time. Bickering bitternesses, dark histories. It's so convoluted that, rather than unravel the detail of power, the plethora of opinions only pulls the knot tighter.

Adi Litia Cakobau is one of the names. Daughter of the last king, with a heritage back to the first. This blood, very distantly, will be that of my grandchild, and the reason I'm permitted on the island today. A coup plotter? Her sister, Adi Samanunu Cakobau, Ambassador to Malaysia, Speight reveals as his choice for Prime Minister. I want someone to point them out, but no one can find them. When I put their names later to a contact in Suva, he shakes his head. Supporters, yes, but not organisers. He gives me a different name. Ilesa Duvuloco, Nationalist Party leader. A coup plotter? He nods rhythmically. Who knows? On the day of the coup, Duvuloco's son stole the Prime Minister's Korean four-wheel drive, and took off for a joy ride to Nausori, a town on the cusp of Tailevu, the largest province in Kubuna confederacy.

My first night in the country, a woman offers me a tatty photocopy. It is a frightening list of bad deeds, including murder. Ratu Mara, my informant explains. Disinformation? Kubuna? No question. There is no sign of him at the funeral among the Lau Group delegation. Yet, through strategic marriages his blood runs thick in Bau. And that's another rub. These blood connections between confederacy clans would seem to count for nothing in the face of family rivalries.

Key faces are missing, and it's becoming awkward to ask for more. But I am encouraged to believe they are here. Perhaps it is my imagination, but there is a smell in the air, on this day of farewell, of unclean affiliations and shifting powers. An unlikely mix, here from all over the country, will whisper not a word of the grubbiness consuming Fiji. They will enter the church, heads bowed, and sing as one: 'The Sands of Time are Sinking', 'The Lord Is My Shepherd' and 'Now Praise We Great and Famous Men'.

There is one village whose men are the gravediggers for the chiefly families of Bau. After they lower the coffin, they sit on top of and around the lid of the tomb, about 20 of them, their hands behind their backs, and pass between them the bitter leaf of the *kura*, each taking a bite before giving it over to the next, around and around. After the ceremony, I follow

COUP

their irregular file down to the sea. Fully clothed and with shouts and guffaws, they dive in. A customary ritual cleansing.

As I snap away at their ungodly yahooing in the water, questions trickle to mind. I had listened earlier in the day to two old women disapprove the slipping of tradition. Next to them sat a young boy pumping recklessly at PlayStation. I thought, as I switched from one to the other, is custom as tightly woven into the Fijian psyche as some would have you believe? Or is a new world claiming the minds of the next generation? And will it be this generation who will rattle the tired old power bases seen mourning this afternoon?

Back in Suva, I settle in between the block walls of my motel room to read a couple of pages passed to me about the intricacies of Speight's dubious mahogany business dealings. As I wearily skim the type, it crosses my mind, how intact has remained the independence of the judiciary? Has it come out of this debacle as well? After all, it has written decrees for the military, which is less than a good sign. And a military tainted by its early inaction has been there for the world to see. When I put this to a Fijian lawyer the next day, he says that the Chief Justice will be pragmatic, not academic. There's the answer. I ask how then will the judiciary respond to a court challenge on the setting aside of the 1997 Constitution, keeping in mind that the Constitution has yet to be legally abrogated? The reply is succinct. The Chief Justice will appoint the judge. Nothing here to warm a deposed Prime Minister's heart.

I move to Ba in the west, where Chaudhry was born, and to the cane fields where the Indians first came into this unbalanced equation. They immigrated under a dreadful indentured labour system that impelled many of their young men to suicide. My eldest daughter's partner, the Indo-Fijian, lived here as a kid. He said they have a very good soccer team.

'I want to talk to someone about the coup,' I say to several earnest young men seated randomly about a front office. After a lengthy silence, one of them points to a chair. I have stumbled across the Ba headquarters of both the Fiji Labour Party and the Federated Farmers' Union (Chaudhry was once the union's secretary). It looks like a small disused shop. The names of both organisations, in red block type, are on the front window.

From the back emerges a large Indian man who introduces himself as Gaffar Ahmed, assistant Minister of Home Affairs in the Coalition government. 'Were you not taken hostage?' I ask. He was, but signed away his position in return for his early release by Speight. In Ba, he has forfeited respect for doing so.

I ask him what Chaudhry did wrong, and he sets forth on a long list of what Chaudhry did right. Staple food prices down, the electricity rate down, the water rate down, mortgage interest rates down, free education up to form five (previously form three), good socially responsible stuff. Chaudhry maintained investor confidence, Ahmed says, and he recites a number of hotel projects, jobs for 4000 workers. I try again for what Chaudhry did wrong, but Ahmed has an engagement now with the young men still in his office, all of whom are leaning forward in their short sleeves, intent on our conversation.

I set out for the cane fields with a farm advisory officer from the Fiji Sugar Company. An Indian. Forty-two of his extended family now live in Canada, including his eldest daughter who will become a doctor. He and his wife will remain to face the challenge, as he puts it, of this latest reversal, although she smiles coyly at her reluctance. Their remaining three children will study hard, then leave. In a country that sees them as second-class citizens, 'guests' who must act accordingly, it is hardly a surprise that Indian students display a greater desire for educational success than Fijian. It will be their way out.

A short and middle-aged shopkeeper from Ba turns up, as arranged, at my hotel. We drive a little way out of town to visit a long-retired Indian civil servant, someone who was close to Mara, he tells me. We pass cane farms once leased by Punjabis and Gujaratis who, he continues, understood very well the tangle of obstacles ahead. They left for the United States, even before the last coup. Indians and Fijians are much closer in the west, anyone will tell you, and the shopkeeper tells me now. Not quite blood brothers, but there are not the same resentments as those wafting about east of Viti Levu. While there is some truth in this, not far into any conversation, even in the west, each side pops out a stereotypical contempt for the other. He does, too. Put simply: Fijians are lazy and Indians want only money. Neither is true, but these dearly held trademarks have come to define the cultural abyss separating the two races.

We drink *kava* from modest enamel bowls, while several toads clean up the insects on the civil servant's verandah. He speaks at length about Fijian history, from cannibalism and missionaries to girmit and sugar companies. I listen and take notes, but I'm impatient for him to land at current events. When he does, what he has to say is astonishing. The two races, he says quietly, cannot continue with parallel development. It has not worked, and will not work. Either the two integrate — by this he means inter-marry, become one — or the Indians must leave. *The Indians must leave.*

On the ride back to my hotel, we pass a Hindu temple nestled amongst the tall sugar cane, and an elegant mosque in the middle of town, symbols that make the integration he speaks of impossible to presume. The Indians must leave? Was he pulling my leg? His parting statement through the car window was that the Indian population will reduce from its current 43 to 30 per cent. That made more sense.

The roads are diabolical as we negotiate the grassroots of Chaudhry's support. And it is here, among the deposed Prime Minister's staunchest supporters, loyal to the core, that a picture begins to develop. The water man dispenses cool water from a large aluminium teapot for the cane cutters scattered about, resting on the discarded leaves of the cane they have just cut. The sweat runs freely from them. They earn seven dollars a day, and not one wouldn't vote for Chaudhry again. As we talk more, however, from farm to farm, field to field, man after man admits to apprehension with Chaudhry's installation as Prime Minister. When asked why, most grimace: arrogance. The toughest, most intelligent and successful trade unionist in the country. They knew, only too well, that many of Fiji's dethroned powerful, to which you must attach a few wealthy Indian businessmen, would not cope with a socialist Prime Minister, an Indian Prime Minister and, in particular, this Indian. May 19 came as no surprise.

On the front porch of the Ba Hotel, I ask the Indian manager, 'Are the powerful in Fiji so abysmally intolerant that the brashness of a single Indian can lead to a coup? Or is it something else?' He purses his lips and shrugs.

I climb aboard an inter-city bus and aim for Suva, but the road ahead is anything but clear. An hour and a half into the journey, the bus pulls into Rakiraki, near the top of Viti Levu, along the Kings Road. The driver turns off the engine, stopping the Bollywood video short of its climax. There is a great deal of excited talk. Another bus pulls up alongside, just in from Suva, and a little melee forms beneath my open window. The short of it is, there's a rebel roadblock at Korovou, in Tailevu country, Speight's supporters, about two hours further on. The bus alongside was the last to make it through. They hijacked the earlier one form our end and robbed the passengers, the Indian ticket man says.

We have a choice, he gravely explains. Stay in Rakiraki and get a full refund of your fare, or take the bus back, and you will have nothing more to pay. I opt for the second, after dropping thoughts of a taxi to the roadblock to see what is going on. Civil unrest can wait until tomorrow. I bus many hours in the opposite direction, and reach Suva in the dark, half an hour before curfew.

I offer to keep Jone Dakuvula's name out of the story, but he says it's okay. Dakuvula was the one who bad-mouthed Speight and his group on television, and 10 minutes later a mob ransacked the station. They just missed Dakuvula, who had had the presence of mind to leave quickly. On the advice of a friend, he slept away from home that night.

I want to know, how did the SVT react? This was Rabuka's party, the one sponsored by the Great Council of Chiefs, and supported by the ultra-nationalist Taukei Movement, the big losers at the polls in 1999. Dakuvula was on the inside, you could say. Although he's now with the Citizens Constitutional Forum (their motto: *one nation, diverse peoples*), and even once, way back, an organising secretary in Chaudhry's Fiji Labour Party, for years he was a media adviser in Rabuka's Prime Minister's office. The new leader of the new Opposition brought him in as a close adviser. Dakuvula resigned, disillusioned, three months after he began.

This is what he tells me. Their crushing defeat at the hands of this Indian shocked the many SVT Members of Parliament who had lost their seats. At their angry post-election meeting, they told Rabuka there must be a military coup, but Rabuka refused, swearing by the 1997 Constitution, and resigned. A rabble-rousing speech later by their new leader, Ratu Inoke Kubuabola, demands that the life of the People's Coalition government be shortened, and 'if blood is to be shed, we must prepare for it'.

'I was quite surprised when I heard this,' says Dakuvula. 'They were talking about kidnap, burning, a coup, murder. And they were serious. Given the army or weapons, they would do it.'

The army command declined, so it goes, but a group of its Special Forces stepped forward, and offered the coup plotters the military coercion they needed. The rest of the army held together under Commodore Bainimarama, their commander, when the potential for it to spin out of control must have been enormous. It restrained its muscle, declaring a peaceful solution paramount. The hostages were the key. But Dakuvula puts another spin on it. The army, he says, split about 70/30 in favour of the commander. With a wrong move, that cut could have turned around completely. The army, he explains, is very professional, well trained, well disciplined, very able. However, in the context of Fijian events, some of that goes out the window, and other communal concerns count for more. The recent shoot-out, and mass arrest of Speight and his supporters, would seem to have called that bluff. But I'm not so sure. Like the judiciary, the army hasn't come out of this well.

It is early evening, warm but not hot, and we are at a small table on my hotel balcony. Dakuvula balances on the edge of his chair, and talks of a committee formed soon after the election defeat, within the SVT, to destabilise the new government. The Nationalist Party joined these shadowy meetings, and so, too, did a small group from the Fijian Association Party, grumpy that Chaudhry had neglected to consult them on who should become Prime Minister. Predictably, they had coveted their party leader, a Fijian. Perhaps foolishly, they did not assemble until the Tuesday following the election, by which time Chaudhry was Prime Minister. And so the disinformation campaign began, a mean-spirited crusade to put Chaudhry and democracy where they are today.

He was always going to be up against it, Dakuvula explains, if only because he was Indian. But he didn't help himself. Dakuvula hands me an example to make it clear. His son had regularly screeched, quite rightly, of nepotism in the previous government. Yet one of Chaudhry's first moves as Prime Minister was to appoint his son as his private secretary. To top that, says Dakuvula, the son had even more lip than the father. Fijian misgivings soared.

What else? He rejected out of hand the conditions set by the SVT to join his Cabinet, as they had a right to do under a peculiar electoral system that allows the Opposition, the losers, to have seats in Cabinet. Immovable. In one breath, he legitimised the cause of the very people who aimed to do him harm. Forget his social and economic policies, they meant nothing to these people.

His Land Use Commission, Dakuvula explains, became another cripplingly misguided political move. Very responsibly, it tackled the pressing land issues hopelessly neglected by previous (Fijian) governments. But instead of paying due respect to two crucial institutions, the Great Council of Chiefs and the Native Lands Trust Board, the commission by-passed them, choosing instead to deal directly with the landowners, and alienation — particularly of the head of the NLTB, Marika Qarikau — that could not have been more complete.

I walk with Dakuvula downstairs to his car. On the way back up, I ponder the dark forces he has to old me about. If the names he has given me are correct, they are a bunch as mixed as those in 1987. Some of them genuinely believe multiracial democracy (and Chaudhry) to be a threat to the well-being of indigenous Fijians. They've been at it a long time. But others have hidden behind the image of selfless fighters for the indigenous cause, when their truth is elsewhere. How could a whole groundswell of Fijians be convinced, by those with other agendas, that Chaudhry's master plan for Fiji was 'a little India'? And why didn't Chaudhry counter the crass disinformation campaign? Is he a politician or not?

Sick of it all, I slip back into New Zealand to await my grandson's birth. He comes three weeks early; 6lb 8oz. I stand with his Fijian father and laugh about Speight and his group being hostages of the military on an island once a quarantine for indentured Indians. They have done their dirty work. But what of the powerful behind them? I lunch with Brij Lal, one of three architects of the 1997 Constitution, at the home of the Indo-Fijian parents of my eldest daughter's partner. We talk of the same things.

From their hill suburb, I look out to Wellington harbour and struggle to imagine them ever having lived in the places I've just been to. Flickering pictures transport me back to the Fiji military's nightly spokesman on television, and a word he repeats like a mantra: *normalcy*.

It crashed around in my head because Fiji is where my grandson and my daughter and her partner will have to live, at least some of their lives. A return to *normalcy*? What he means is an end to violence. Not a return to the elected government. Not a return to democracy.

LIVING IN UNUSUAL TIMES

Sir Vijay R. Singh

1. Living in Unusual Times

We live in unusual times, almost like Alice in Wonderland, where things are seldom what they seem or are claimed to be.

Most of us have friends of all races — many of them very close and almost like members of the family — but at this tense hour we do not know on whose integrity to the rule of law, commitment to uphold the constitution and concepts of decency we can really rely.

Most of those whom we had chosen as our leaders in calm times on the strength of their self-advertised commitment to champion democracy and protect the people's rights, although not held hostage, suddenly discovered after 19 May that they suffered from uncontrollable diarrhoea that constrained them to remain close to their closets, or that their acute laryngitis infection precluded them from speaking out on behalf of the people they had chosen to represent.

Or had other urgent commitments elsewhere.

Discretion, according to the politically correct, may well be the better part of valour, but it is also symptomatic of cowardice, examples of which we have now witnessed in ample measure.

While a select few had the courage to state their convictions, even if others disagreed with their expressions, the vast numbers of a select group of honourable men and women who basked in the community's adulation and respect in good times are suddenly missing or silent when the people face the most traumatic time of our lives.

Meanwhile, many a well-fed lily-livered religious leader lectures us to love our assailants and forgive the destroyers of our livelihood.

Not surprisingly, Ilisoni Ligairi, a retired soldier of distinction, has emerged as the real power behind the throne and controller of events that began six weeks ago, thereby destroying the shadow of the myth that it was a 'civilian coup'.

So we come back to square one — the official military versus its own kith and kin, the serving and former soldiers who have been on extra-curricular duties at the parliamentary complex for the last six weeks that Commodore Bainimarama has to deal with.

How it resolves this situation will demonstrate the mettle of the official military and the reason for its existence.

2. The Skylark will Sing

It has been well said before.

Nobel Laureate Rabindra Nath Tagore in *Gitanjali* expressed well where we aspired to head for:

Where the mind is without fear and the head is held high
Where knowledge is free
Where the world has not been broken up into fragments
By narrow domestic wall
Where words come out from the depth of truth
Where tireless striving stretches its arms towards perfection
Where the clear stream of reason has not lost its way
Into the dreary desert sand of dead habit
Where the mind is led forward by thee
Into ever widening thought and action
Into that heaven of freedom, my Father, let my country awake.

And some years later His Holiness Pope John Paul III visited us and declared, 'Fiji, The Way the World Should Be'. We were getting there, for sure.

But in 1987 and more grievously again last May, the passion for power on the part of some moved them to treason and hold prisoner not only their government but their reason and religion, as well.

On each occasion, most customary and chosen leaders said they were unaware of their people's aspirations until the coup makers told them so — whereupon they readily agreed and gave earnest encouragement to evil deeds.

But in so doing, they ignored the wise counsel of Khalil Gibran:

Your reason and your passion are the rudder and the sails of your
*   seafaring soul.*
If either your sails or your rudder be broken, you can but toss and drift,
Or else be held at standstill in mid seas.
For reason, ruling alone is a force confining.
And passion, unattended, is a flame that burns its own destruction.
Therefore, let your soul exalt your reason to the height of passion,
That it may sing:
And let it direct your passion with reason
That your passion may live through its own daily resurrection
And, like the phoenix, rise above its own ashes.

While those who lusted for undeserved power — and their many misguided followers — were embarked upon a malignant enterprise against their homeland and its leaders, most successors to ancient warriors and the ethically naked but finely attired retailers of divine wisdom sank deeper into the ashes of their own vice.

They sought reflected glory in glorifying the inhumanity of their sinful flock; but in their uncompassionate hearts could not find the will to spare a moment to cast a comforting glance at the hapless and innocent prey who languished but a few yards away.

They joined together to desecrate the national motto — Fear God and Honour the Chief — for they violated the solemn promise.

And their political outriders, far and wide, high and low, military and civilian, hastened to proclaim their support for the newly invented 'cause', while occasionally proclaiming not to support the evil means — at least for the record — nevertheless, had not the courage to condemn and resist it.

Some enacted the charade of seeking forgiveness of their victims but without showing a semblance of remorse for the evil they had wrought, claiming that this was their custom and tradition.

Such pretence of piety will not heal the trauma of the hostages and their loved ones for their 55-day stopover into hell. Or wash away the tears of Filipo Seavula's young wife suddenly made widow or her young orphaned son, or diminish the daily agony of parents, suddenly made jobless, as they strive to feed their hungry children.

Some of the victims may, in a show of genuine or simulated generosity of spirit, feign forgiveness.

As for me,

I am no Homer's Hero, you all know,
I profess not Generosity to a Foe.
My Generosity is to my Friends,
That for their Friendship I may make amends.
The Generous to Enemies promotes their ends
And becomes the Enemy and Betrayer of his Friends.

Because, as Martin Luther King Jr said:

I am coming to feel that the people of ill will have used time much more effectively than the people of goodwill.

Undeserved forgiveness is unforgivable encouragement of evil.

But all who gloat at the triumph of lawlessness and its perceived prizes might do well to heed Bob Dylan's 1963 lyrics in his *Song for the Rocks in the Stream*:

The line it is drawn; the curse it is cast
The slow one now will later be fast
As the present now will later be past
The old order is rapidly fading
And the first one now will later be last
For the times, they are a-changing.

The already sidelined and discriminated and soon to be displaced Indo-Fijians now know that their ethnic Fijian friends and neighbours, 'they are a-changing, and the line is drawn and the curse is cast'.

But however distressed and disillusioned, they will behave as they always have — with the same patience and fortitude that their forefathers showed in the long night of the '*Girmit*' — 'With a mind without fear and head held high'.

As Khalil Gibran said with touching eloquence:

You can muffle the drum,
You can loosen the strings of the lyre,
But who shall command the skylark
Not to sing.

It has indeed, all been well said before.

3. Uneasy Answers

With each passing day, the crisis that we have endured for seven long weeks seems to have become increasingly complex, with the potential for much more devastating consequences than have already been visited upon our hapless people. An event that was originally regarded as an act of terrorism, hostage taking and treason by a civilian-led posse of serving and retired soldiers has unravelled in most peculiar ways.

There are no easy answers to any hostage crisis, but the manner in which events have unfolded — or been permitted to unfold — serve to perplex most people and pain others.

One assumes that the military, and the police force, too, led as it is by a former senior army officer, had some idea of the 'cockpit drill' to follow immediately such a crisis eventuates.

Elsewhere in the world, the parliamentary complex would have been immediately cordoned off, making it off-limits to civilians, and all communication between the hostage takers and the outside world cut off.

But that is not the Fiji way.

A large human shield has been allowed to establish itself at Parliament. Hundreds of supporters have been allowed to visit and offer gifts of food and encouragement to the hostage takers, who themselves are allowed to give press interviews and to go to a TV studio to debate the army. And, according to a rumour, in the early days, to shower and change at the barracks before resuming their extra-curricular duties at Parliament, although this might be a bit far-fetched.

All the while national leaders who are victims of the crime have languished in lonely silence for seven long weeks.

Is that the Fiji way?

The Council of Chiefs took a whole day to decide the obvious — to give the President its unequivocal support — only to undermine the President's executive authority the next day by deciding to negotiate with George Speight, one of whose demands was the President's removal from office.

Is that the Fiji way?

The President dismissed the Government and assumed executive authority. The military leaders then stepped up and asked him, who was then the Government and Commander in Chief, to step aside and go visit his farm in Lakeba. They did so in the 'traditional way', although it is not clear when that tradition was established. And the President, surprisingly, obeyed.

That was a coup of sorts. By consent; the Fiji way.

When it assumed executive authority on 29 May 2000, the military posture gave the impression that it knew what needed to be done to release the hostages, and knew also, how to do it.

It therefore 'wholly removed' the Constitution; abolished the Supreme Court, dismissed members of the Public Service Commission and countermanded the appointment of two Indo-Fijians as ambassadors and offered the hostage takers amnesty.

If that was an uniquely Fiji way to obtain the hostages' release, it didn't work.

In the meantime arms were removed from the FMF armoury and found their way into the care and custody of the hostage takers and their sympathisers. Was this an example of military security, the Fiji way?

The military then began interminable negotiations with George Speight on the future of Fiji, a profound matter on which neither side has any authority, and arrived at the Muanikau Accord. It remains a secret document although it affects every member of the public in profound ways, including those not yet born.

Eventually, the President's secretary Joe Brown announced that 'the journey' (not the agony) that had begun on 19 May would end the next day. But it was not to be. Mr Ligairi vetoed the Accord.

Having possibly given away much that was non-negotiable, the 'negotiations' came to naught. But the offer of amnesty remains.

In between, military leaders kept expressing their sympathy for the hostage takers' objectives. To test that sympathy, two junior officers at the Labasa barracks led a mutiny and held hostage their superior, giving further proof of the breakdown in discipline in the principal arm of the disciplined forces.

And while chiefs and hundreds of their men rushed to the barracks to lend the mutineers their support, the military top brass negotiated with its own rebellious soldiers.

Is that leadership by example, the Fiji way?

In the meantime, civilian factions got in the act. One wanted the military to vacate its Nabua headquarters. Another closed Labasa airport. Another still, rather fittingly under the circumstances, visited darkness on much of the country by messing about with the Monasavu electricity supply.

Is that too the Fiji way?

In the meantime, the long hour of darkness engulfing the lives of the hostages and their loved ones receives scant attention.

And now voices are raised against Commodore Bainimarama; that he too must go. Might he be asked to do so in 'the traditional way'? Or the military way?

All the while, the Indo-Fijians, the declared 'enemy', lick their wounded souls in silence and, like the ill-starred hostages, wondered — when will this hideous nightmare end? Or are we on the threshold of much worse — the 'Fiji way'?

4. Role Models for the Young

Much has been said about the traumatic events that began on 19 May sending the economy rushing downhill. But in our preoccupation with material values we have paid scant attention to a much more substantial and grievous impoverishment that has already diminished us as a people and will assuredly impair the quality of our relationship with our neighbours, even after the economy has been rehabilitated.

No society can afford to allow individuals or groups among it to defy the rules of conduct that all are required to observe in the larger interest of the well-being, and even survival, of the community as a whole.

That is the reason why parliaments make laws, the police prosecute suspected offenders and courts punish the guilty and prisons incarcerate them. All these things are done to advance the welfare of society as a whole and deter lawlessness.

Those who hold offices in the state apparatus are accorded respect and obedience for what they do in society's interest. We hold them out as role models for our children and encourage them to follow in the footsteps of the pillars of society and be worthy citizens of whom we may be proud parents.

Painful experience has shown to civilised societies the world over that lawlessness becomes endemic if some are held to be above the law of the land because, after all, it's the laws that bind individuals and groups together to make a composite society. Further, society makes punishment fit the crime; the more serious the lawlessness, the more severe the penalty.

Once leaders of any society adopt the posture that some persons are above the law or that certain crimes should be forgiven because they were committed for an acceptable objective, they invite repeated acts of lawlessness by others for similar objectives. From there on, it's a slippery downhill road.

Let us be frank and look real ty in the face, however unpalatable it might be.

Lieutenant Colonel Sitiveni Rabuka, as he then was, barged into our consciousness in 1987 by holding government Members of Parliament hostage, deposing the Queen as Head of State and abrogating the Constitution. As he has candidly admitted, he and his collaborators had committed treason, the most heinous crime known to law.

Instead, half the country treated him as a hero if not its saviour. Leaders granted him amnesty, made him a life member of the Great Council of Chiefs, promoted him in the army and propelled him to the road to elective leadership of the country.

Although those who got to know him later found Rabuka to be a charming and intelligent person who, by his own admission, had been used by others to commit the coup, the fact that he was rewarded with amnesty and later enjoyed political success had its own dynamics. He paved the way for George Speight and his group of rebellious civilians and former and serving army officers to embark on a similar escapade for the same objective — indigenous Fijian supremacy.

On this occasion, an impotent army has readily granted Speight and all his supporters amnesty for their 'political' crimes since 19 May and any that they might commit for several days thereafter.

The way in which so many leaders and rank and file members of the ethnic Fijian community have rushed to his support has certainly transformed George Speight into an overnight folk hero. And these parents hold him out as a role model for their children to follow when they become adults.

But it is not George Speight alone that one should be concerned about. The amnesty granted by military leaders to rebellious and mutinous soldiers will only encourage their likes, including children still at school, not to fear acting in like manner.

They are the real victims of the painful drama that has been our daily companion since mid-May.

Perhaps the next hostage-takers might, as in Labasa, be junior soldiers, mutinying against their superiors. Or school children may practise it on their teachers, and workers on their employers and prisoners on their guards.

On the basis of precedent, they too will, understandably, expect forgiveness without remorse, and amnesty from prosecution and punishment for their misdeeds.

Those who have sown the seeds of a culture of lawlessness in pursuit of a purportedly righteous cause have done our future generations incalculable disservice. And it will beget grief to all for decades to come.

WHO WILL PICK UP
THE PIECES?

Daryl Tarte

Over the past weeks as the devastating consequences of the events of 19 May have begun to have their real impact on the nation, I have been trying to rationalise my own reactions. I suppose my overpowering emotion is one of anger. Anger, that a small group of armed men should have the arrogance to proclaim that they know what is best for our people and our country. Anger, that they apparently have no care or consideration for the disastrous consequences of their actions.

But the other dominant emotion is one of sadness. Sadness, that the aspirations and hopes of so many people, and of a nation collectively, should be shattered so abruptly. Sadness, about the fear and suffering that the people of this nation must now endure and the terrible economic hardships that lie ahead.

Sadness, that law and order have given way to anarchy.

Whenever I see our Pacific blue flag fluttering at the masthead, I remember with great poignancy that day in Albert Park 30 years ago when it was unfurled for the first time and the hearts of every Fiji citizen swelled with pride and hope. I recall Ratu Sir Kamisese Mara pointedly reminding us that we were not celebrating the end of British rule but the beginning of self-rule.

That flag still flies and remains a symbol of our freedom. It represents the lovely islands of Lau and the Yasawas; the rich delta flats of Nadi and Ba; the lush jungles of Taveuni, the clean air that we breathe. It represents freedom from persecution and the right to vote and speak our

coup

91

views. It represents the brotherhood of Fijians and Indians, Europeans and Chinese, Rotumans and Melanesians, Muslims and Hindus, Catholics and Protestants. It represents hard work and thrift. It represents freedom of assembly, tolerance and understanding. It represents honesty, trust and sharing.

Some will say that the hope which filled our hearts on 10 October 1970 has not been fulfilled; that unacceptable disparities have arisen between the races; that in trying to keep pace with globalisation we have lost our way; that in attempting to impose western democracy we have sacrificed traditional values; that Fijians have been in danger of losing control in the land of their ancestors. These claims contain elements of truth. Yet, despite the imperfections, our systems were dealing more effectively than most other countries with similar problems.

Perhaps our very success has been the cause of our downfall. Perhaps we have been so concerned with economic growth that we became insensitive to the rumblings of discontent that were simmering malignantly in our bowels.

We allowed the flag to become faded and tattered. No one cared so long as there was money in the bank and time for leisure. Patriotism was regarded as something we need not waste time upon. We treated 10 October as a holiday rather than an opportunity to rededicate ourselves to Fiji, or as a time to honestly re-examine our progress and determine whether the objectives of self-rule were being achieved. People only thought of Fiji collectively when we won the Hong Kong sevens.

Now, the malignant growth that we could have treated has erupted into a suppurating sore that is slowly poisoning the whole Fiji body. There remains no pride in being a Fiji citizen. Only sadness as the fabric of life crumbles. The world mocks us and writes us off as just another basket case.

We must not allow this!

Our island nation has always had the ingredients to build, not a nation of power, nor one of strategic importance, but one where its people can have a satisfactory degree of prosperity and be happy. We have our share of natural resources and a unique mix of cultures. We have in our midst men and women of the utmost integrity and intellectual ability. We have demonstrated that we can be an example to the rest of the world.

Let us not squander these marvellous gifts.

It is time for our collective human resource to be harnessed and for true leaders who have the interests of the whole country and of all people, as their utmost priority, to come forth and vigorously and steadfastly uphold justice and the dignity of all men and women of this nation. It is incumbent on all the diverse people who profess to be citizens of this country to be upstanding, support those leaders, and proclaim their loyalty to the country of their ancestors or adoption. That huge silent group must become the vocal majority.

I am reminded of Ratu Seru Cakobau's statement to Sir Hercules Robinson at the signing of the Deed of Cession at Levuka 126 years ago. 'What of the future?' he asked rhetorically. 'If things remain as they are, Fiji will become like a piece of driftwood on the sea and be picked up by the first passer-by.'

My third emotion is according v one of fear. Fear, about the way we are drifting aimlessly into a sea of intrigue and turmoil. Fear, about who will pick up the pieces of driftwood

16

FIJI VILLAGERS' BUS TRIP TO FREEDOM

Phil Thornton

The Indo-Fijian villagers of Muaniweni have been terrorised and beaten by masked men from the village of Muamua in the Fiji Islands. Local police, media and army have failed to protect them. Helped by donations from a Suva-based group of humanitarians, they have decided to flee their homes. The villagers asked journalist Phil Thornton to join them on their flight to safety.

The villagers of Muaniweni have had enough. Since Fiji rebel leader George Speight's armed coup, masked men have terrorised them, battered them, stolen their possessions, killed their farm animals and trashed their homes.

Now the villagers say they can't take any more of the violence so they're leaving. They have taken advantage of the long weekend to break out.

They've been briefed to tell military roadblocks that they are on their way to a religious ceremony in Nadi.

'We lost our security ... we can't live here,' says villager Rudra Deo, whose wife had a razor-sharp axe held to her throat by a masked man demanding money from her, or they'd rape her.

'If we hear a dog bark we're frightened. We can't sleep. We can't eat. So much damage has been done to our village and we've had no protection from the police or the army,' he says sadly.

Many of the villagers are crying as they file slowly onto the large, single-decker bus, hired by concerned people in Suva, to take 72 villagers to a safe sanctuary in Lautoka on the western side of Viti Levu.

This will be Fiji's first refugee camp and is set up in the grounds of the Lautoka Sanatan Primary School.

The men, women and children are dressed in donated clothing and look as if they're going on a Sunday outing.

But the packed bus is silent. Deadly quiet.

Children aren't laughing. Women quietly weep and men stare blankly. Bulging suitcases and string-tied cardboard boxes jam the aisle.

'We've left everything behind. we just turned our animals loose, I've got three young children to think of,' says Deo.

The villagers explain that armed masked men still wander around the village at night making noises.

The bus kicks up clouds of dust as it bounces down the hills and slowly edges its way up them as it makes its way over 20 kilometres of unsealed road to the main road. The bus has to cover a slow 260 kilometres before it reaches Lautoka.

Every military roadblock the bus passes increases the tension for the villagers. And they almost lose it completely at Pacific Harbour, on the outskirts of Suva, when a policeman runs from the station and waves the bus to stop.

Panic sweeps through the villagers as the policeman and driver talk. To the relief of the passengers the bus is waved on.

The driver explains that a family who was meant to join the bus at Suva had phoned the police station to leave a message to say they would make their own way to Lautoka.

Many of the villagers have never been away from Muaniweni before, explains James Chandra. 'We only ever leave the village for weddings or ceremonies, then it's all noise, music and laughter. Look at us — we're so sad.'

Village shopkeeper Subhash Chand, 23, was in his house with his grandmother, mother and father when the masked men starting smashing their front door with cane knives.

COUP

'I had an iron bar and a knife, but when I saw how many there were, I dropped my knife and my knees wouldn't stop shaking.'

The masked men told Subhash that if he stayed in his house they would burn it with him in it.

'I was angry but what could I do. They hit me with the cane knife, but I fell and it broke the impact. They kicked and punched me. Most of the attackers were my customers,' he says shaking his head.

The people don't expect any help from the authorities. According to trainee teacher Amitesh Chandra, 19, the villagers feel the local media has let them down.

'When we needed them to come and photograph our houses they never came, now we have to leave our homes and seek sanctuary from people in the west,' says an angry Amitesh.

The bus winds around the edges of the Coral Coast passing holiday resorts popular with Australian holiday-makers: Naviti, Warwick and the Hideaway.

As they get further from Suva, the villagers relax and start to talk. Finally, the bus pulls up in front of the gates of the Lautoka Sanatan Primary Scool, but because of its size is unable to enter. The villagers spill from the bus carrying their boxes and suitcases.

Young boys are struggling with bags and old women carrying religious artifacts.

Within minutes of the classrooms being opened the women have found straw brushes and are cleaning the floors. The men move the benches and desks from the rooms. Children have found the swings and slides in the playground and are laughing.

'Our women and children are really happy to be safe,' says a pleased Amitesh.

As word gets out on the 'coconut telegraph' of the refugees' arrival, curious locals start to stream into the school grounds.

When the locals hear the villagers' stories there's much shaking of heads, tears and anger.

'We have to protect these people. We'll give them food, shelter anything they need we'll find it for them,' says local chef, Edward John.

Another local says Indo-Fijians and Fijians in the west get on and there's no problem here.

While groups of enthusiastic locals go off to organise mattresses, blankets and food, the villagers call a meeting. Dr Roy Krishna, head of School of Health Sciences at the Fiji School of Medicine, talks to the older villagers about the importance of taking their prescribed medications. He says it's crucial their health is monitored and local doctors have offered to come by in the morning to do so.

'Many of these people will suffer mental trauma. It's not only from the physical attacks, but also the lack of security, and emotional shock of leaving their homes and a lifetime of memories behind. All this will erode their mental well-being,' says Dr Krishna.

Rajmaz Avisher carries his young son, Rahil, 8, to Dr Krishna. He explains the frail-looking boy has a congenital heart problem and has to take regular medication and see a specialist.

'It's a big problem for us. I've got three other children and we're really frightened,' says Avisher.

Dr Krishna reassures the father and boy that he will have a doctor look at his son in the morning.

A spokeswoman for the organisers of the freedom bus trip says her group will be looking at bringing in counsellors, family support workers, doctors and legal opinion to help the villagers get back to normal.

A week ago Amitesh Chandra, 19, was a polite young villager, but you get the feeling he's had enough of being kicked around. He's busy organising security for the school grounds and has met with the local police and army.

'The [local] community support is wonderful. The people are very kind. Even the police and the army have promised to protect us. At home in our village we were easy to pick on, here we'll be safe. We're all together,' says a determined Amitesh.

17

GUNS AND MONEY

Mark Revington

Sometimes power in Fiji doesn't come from the barrel of a gun. All it takes is a threat. During the first 10 days of the Fijian coup, some of the best reporting and analysis came from the journalism students at the University of the South Pacific (USP), on their Pacific Journalism Online web site. On the 11th day, the web site was closed down. The previous night, supporters of George Speight had trashed the studio and offices of Fiji Television, following criticism of Speight during a current affairs show.

Pacific Online immediately posted a transcript of the program, with its caustic criticism and political commentator Jone Dakuvula's observation that all the talk about indigenous rights was simply a smokescreen for a naked power grab. And Vice-Chancellor Esekia Solofa immediately closed it down 'as a security measure' after threats were made against the university. (The web site, which had been recording about 20,000 hits a day, was eventually put back in cyberspace, hosted by the journalism department of an Australian university.)

Right there you had the paradox of 'Coup-coup' land (as Australian journalists have dubbed Fiji), encapsulating the two great 'isms' — globalism and tribalism — sweeping the post-Cold War world, detailed by American scholar Benjamin Barber in his book *Jihad vs McWorld*. Look on the business pages of any paper, says Barber, and you would be convinced the world was increasingly united, that borders were increasingly porous. Look only at the front pages and you would be convinced of the opposite; that the world was increasingly riven by fratricide and civil war.

The forces driving the coup were a complex mix, including a class struggle and a reaction against Mahendra Chaudhry's roll-back of privatisation and its opportunities for personal power and lots of loot. Some of the businessmen said to be behind the coup, whose names are on lists circulating in Suva and by email through cyberspace, are all in favour of a free flow of capital as long as it ends up in their pockets. Yet the coup leaders relied for their power base on an insular, tribal intolerance. It was a coup that combined a primitive appeal to indigenous Fijians, with the media savvy of glib frontman Speight. And an echo of colonialism from a gun-toting band supposedly seeking to shake off the colonial shackles. (Threats and censorship are traditional weapons of heavy-handed colonial powers such as France to keep their Pacific colonies in line.)

Although Speight obviously has little regard for democracy, he knows the value of a sound bite only too well, and used the media. In turn, they offered him a profile and credibility. 'They fuelled the crisis and gave Speight a false idea of his importance and support,' says USP senior journalism lecturer David Robie.

Pulled in at the last minute as the great communicator, Speight communicated so well that there is a theory that he mounted a coup within a coup, using his new media profile to get his own way. 'There is a feeling that events didn't unfold the way some people had planned,' says Robie.

Trouble in cyberspace. Robie, who also coordinates Pacific Media Watch, a group dedicated to examining issues of ethics, censorship and media freedom in the Pacific, had been through it before. In 1998, Ministers in then Prime Minister Sitiveni Rabuka's government had tried to close down Robie's own media and politics web site — Café Pacific — and revoke his work permit in what was seen as the first test of the 1997 Constitution's freedom of expression clause. The prime mover was then Assistant Information Minister Ratu Josefa Dimuri, one of Speight's key supporters. The politicians backed off after a two-week media controversy.

An award-winning journalist, and author of seven books, New Zealand-born Robie has been an impassioned chronicler of Pacific currents for decades, an interest developed while working as an editor for the Agence France-Presse news agency in Paris during the early 1970s. After returning to the Pacific in 1977, he began covering Pacific affairs as a freelancer. He witnessed the bloody struggles for independence of the 1980s, and the attempts of independent Pacific nations to chart a nuclear-free course. He reported on the violence between France and Kanak activists in New Caledonia and the massacre of Kanak activists at Hienghene in 1984 that almost provoked a civil war. He was harassed by French secret service agents and arrested at gunpoint by the military in New Caledonia, was on board the *Rainbow Warrior* when it evacuated irradiated Rongelap Islanders from their atoll, leaving the ship one day before it was sunk in Auckland by French secret service agents. He was in Fiji when Dr Timoci Bavadra was elected in 1987, and covered the subsequent coups.

He wrote the book *Blood on Their Banner*, published in 1989, a detailed analysis of the struggle of indigenous people around the Pacific against the remnants of colonialism. The epilogue is just as applicable today in Fiji. 'The death of democracy in Fiji was a blow to many nationalists in the South Pacific, putting the struggle of the Kanaks and other liberation movements in jeopardy,' wrote Robie, who recorded how Rabuka went on a big military spend-up, forging closer ties with France and Indonesia, the two nations so adept at using force to put down indigenous populations in their Pacific colonies.

Thirteen years on and not much seems to have changed in Fiji, says Robie.

'Chauvinistic, nationalistic struggles of this kind, based on nepotism, racism, opportunistic crime, opportunities for corruption and suppression of the human rights of others, undermine genuine indigenous struggles such as the Kanak struggle for independence from France in New Caledonia. After all, Fiji has been independent since 1970. In that time it has had indigenous governments except for one month in 1987 when Bavadra was Prime Minister, and one year in 1999–2000 with Chaudhry.

'What have they done all this time for the underprivileged indigenous villager? Why are they blaming the Chaudhry government after three decades of failure by Mara and Rabuka and the chiefly oligarchy? This is about a Third World oligarchy which has failed its people.'

In another one of those ironies that constantly emerge, both Bavadra's government and that of Chaudhry wanted to help Fiji's poor, often at the expense of cosy business arrangements. Chaudhry may have been too abrasive in his political style, but his heart appeared to be in the right place. His government gave priority to genuine policies to improve health, education and social development.

'It would be fair to say that the Chaudhry government achieved more in one year than the previous Rabuka government achieved in seven years,' says Robie. 'The real problem, not the racial stereotyping which Speight insisted upon, was the roll-back of privatisation and an emphasis on development for the poor.'

Rabuka's former Finance Minister Jim Ah Koy, reputedly one of the richest men in Fiji, was hellbent on privatisation in Fiji, and is one of those rumoured to be behind the coup. The rumours were so strong that Ah Koy felt compelled to make a statement, denying any complicity and launching a vicious attack on Chaudhry. It was run as a full page in all three daily newspapers and read out in full on Fiji Television.

Speight's dubious business dealings have been well documented by the *Sydney Morning Herald*, notably in a piece by Marian Wilkinson headlined 'Mahogany Row', which laid out in detail how Speight, as chairman of the government-backed Fiji Pine Ltd and the Fiji Hardwood Corporation, stood to make a lot of money from the sale of mahogany forests to US interests. Chaudhry's government questioned the price Speight was prepared to accept, end the deal, and sacked him.

Speight also appeared to have been involved in pyramid selling in Queensland, where he spent eight years as an insurance and banking broker.

Fiji, says Robie, is paying the price for years of failure to develop cohesive, homegrown policies to cope with the impact of globalisation. 'Years of corruption, blatant self-interest, short-term band-aid policies, and a neglect of the urban and rural poor communities since independence have taken their toll. It is rare that politicians with vision and genuine selfless commitment to island development have emerged.'

Where to now? Anyone who knew Chaudhry would not have been taken in by his acceptance of kava and a whale's tooth — the traditional Fijian peace offering — from his captors, says Robie. There are Australian and New Zealand judges on the bench in Fiji who are reported to be anticipating a challenge to any new government, not only on legal grounds but also on the grounds that the coup was a violation of the constitutional rights of the Fijian people.

There is an interesting precedent, from Trinidad and Tobago, where the two main ethnic groups are descended from India and Africa. On 27 July 1990, a radical Muslim group took the Prime Minister and Parliament hostage at gunpoint, and stormed the state-run television station. Their leader, Imam Yasin Abu Bakr, declared on national television that he had overthrown the government and consigned them to history. Prime Minister Arthur Robinson was shot in the foot during the six days the government was held hostage, then released to add his authority to a settlement for the release of the hostages. As soon as they were freed, he refused to honour the agreement, saying it had been signed under duress. Over the following months the rebels were arrested and jailed.

CONVERSATIONS AT MAHENDRA CHAUDHRY'S HOME

Jone Dakuvula

Yesterday I was reading an article I received on the internet by Kathy Marks of the *Independent* in the United Kingdom in which she said Major General Sitiveni Rabuka had told her that Colonel Ilisoni Ligairi, Mr Speight's head of security and former head of the elite Counter Revolutionary Warfare Unit, had telephoned the former and said: 'Come here and watch me shoot Mahendra Chaudhry.' I understand that my uncle, Colonel Ligairi, from Nabaletale Village in Wailevu, Cakaudrove, was angry with Rabuka because he had sided with Ratu Sir Kamisese Mara.

This incident prompts me to write about my visit to Mrs Veermati Chaudhry and members of her family at their home at Suva Point on Saturday 21 May. I went to express to her my sympathy and wish that the illegal seizure of her husband's government will be resolved soon. I hope that Mrs Chaudhry will forgive me for revealing here some parts of our conversation but I feel compelled to publish to help public understanding of her and her family members.

I noticed when I entered her kitchen that her family seem to live their private lives, exemplifying what her husband and his political party preaches, that is multiracial tolerance, understanding and peace. They were sitting around the kitchen table listening to the radio. There was her son Sachin, a Fijian woman, an Indo-Fijian woman and two Fijian men. One of the Fijian men is Emosi Bar , Mr Chaudhry's police bodyguard, with whom I had attended Niusawa Methodist Mission School in Taveuni. These were some of the things she told me that I have been thinking about in the last week:

I learnt that the late Mr Frank, an excellent Methodist teacher who taught Emosi Bari and me in Niusawa, was her older brother. Mr Frank had been responsible for looking after the Dilkusha home (just before he retired) and which we heard on the radio had been burnt down.

The first thing Mrs Chaudhry told me was that she wanted the opportunity to forgive those people who were holding her husband hostage and who had threatened his life and physically assaulted him and his son. She also wanted the Government led by her husband to be able to forgive the coup makers after the release. (I think she meant spiritual forgiveness.)

She also said that her husband had often told her and members of his family that what he wanted most to achieve as Prime Minister was to uplift the standard of living of the indigenous Fijian people because they were the community most in need of development. Her husband had told her that he considered it would be the crowning achievement of Mahendra Chaudhry to have Fijians tell him at the end of five years that he had done something significant for them. She said this was a fundamental aim of the Fiji Labour Party Manifesto. (Now, that will be hard to believe especially for those who do not like or who distrust Mahendra Chaudhry, and I include myself amongst such people.)

She regretted that what had happened will tarnish the image of indigenous Fijians all over the world. She said indigenous Fijians did not deserve this image as arrogant racists because what she had experienced in her own life and in her church was that we Fijians were very tolerant, generous and decent Christians.

She observed that it will be very hard for her and members of her family to imagine leaving Fiji as a result of Speight's attempted coup. Their roots, historically and culturally, are so deep and steeped in Fiji, and especially herself, because of her upbringing with indigenous Fijians in the Methodist Church, and now in her new church, the Assemblies of God.

Just before my arrival she told me that a pastor and some members of her church had just left. They had prayed together for all the people in Parliament.

This was the first time for me to meet Mrs Veermati Chaudhry. And she said all this to me in response to my introduction of myself to her as a member of the SVT party who had been a critic of her husband for the last eight years. I spent about an hour in their modest wooden house. It is very clean, neatly furnished with nice furniture and carpet. It has a very homely feeling about it. Now I understand why they did not want to shift. I would not want to shift anywhere else if I had a house, compound and location like theirs.

For a while, we watched the television news of the latest goings-on at the Parliament complex. After hearing George Speight, Sachin and I wondered about his state of mind. Then Emosi Bari expressed his view that the 'coup' was mainly a grab for political power by some leaders of Kubuna who have always believed that they should be politically pre-eminent amongst the indigenous Fijians. Emosi also told me that once he had earnestly advised his boss to include one or two Kubuna Chiefs from the Fijian Association Party backbench in his Cabinet. He had warned Mr Chaudhry that vanua politics was far more dangerous in its power motivation and direction than rivalry between Indian political leaders. The response from his boss was that none of the Fijian Chiefs in the FAP was 'clean' enough to be included.

Mrs Chaudhry told me, at the time I visited, that very few people had been to see them. Mrs Chaudhry's family appeared to be in a cheerful mood when I arrived and when I left. I came away wondering about this gap between my positive impression of the private Chaudhry family and the public image of the Prime Minister that many people have, and that the coup makers said had compelled them to seize his government. Mrs Veermati Chaudhry had impressed me as a dignified and generous woman. Mahendra Chaudhry was a very fortunate man in that regard. I regret that I had not said sorry to her as an indigenous Fijian for what happened to her husband and son.

I join Taufa Vakatale, the former President of the SVT party, and her group of women who had written to Veermati Chaudhry and publicly apologised to her for what had been done to her husband by some of our fellow indigenous Fijians, claiming to be acting in our interest. I also apologise to her for the bad things I have said about her husband to many of my friends and which she does not know.

If there is any reader out there who feels that she or he wants to write to Mrs Veermati Chaudhry, send your letter to her C/– GPO Box 11549, Suva. Let us begin to walk the path of reconciliation that Mrs Chaudhry has shown to us by her own example, now.

FIJI'S NEW WESTERN CONFEDERACY

Roderick Ewins

At the time of British colonisation, there existed three large confederacies, in Fijian called *matanitu*. They were a result of geographical propinquity, kinship ties (often engineered by strategic marriages), and conquests and/or military alliances. They were called *Kubuna* (grouped around the powerful island kingdom of Bau), *Tovata e Viti* (formed by a 19th-century alliance of two smaller confederacies, Cakaudrove and Lau), and *Burebasaga* (grouped around Rewa). The central highlands of the main island of Viti Levu, and the west and northwest, were not traditionally part of these confederacies, but the colonial government found their hierarchies far easier to both comprehend and administer, so the many smaller separate 'western' socio-political entities were simply 'written in' to *Kubuna*, and to a lesser extent into *Burebasaga*. Being 'drafted' into the eastern confederacies has never sat easily with western Fijians, who continue to have significant linguistic, political and cultural differences from eastern Fijians. But the problems were masked during the colonial era by the fact that administration did not directly employ these divisions, instead establishing a system of provinces and districts which they administered by a mixture of direct and indirect rule.

However, because of colonial governmental policies (in particular the power it vested in the Great Council of Chiefs, itself constructed by the first Governor to provide himself with an efficient channel of communication to both seek information and transmit his vice-regal commands), the confederacies continued to be very important power-blocs. Chiefly marriages between them have been used to consolidate dynastic power, and since independence in 1970, the so-called 'Bau/Lau' grouping have tended to dominate Fijian politics. Ratu Sir George Cakobau of Bau became the first Governor-General, with Ratu Sir Kamisese Mara (paramount chief of Lau) as Prime Minister for nearly two decades. Ratu Sir Penaia Ganilau, paramount of Cakaudrove (Lau's partner in the Tovata) next became Governor-General, and after the 1987 coups the President, replaced in turn by Mara. Mara's wife is the highest-ranked chief of Rewa, but Burebasaga has fared less well in the power-stakes than have Bau and Lau, and foreign aid, hurricane relief etc. have long been directed into the east to a degree other Fijians have complained was most inequitable. Western leaders have held none of the strategic posts until the election in 1987 of Bavadra, member of a noble lineage and married to a chief, Adi Kuini (recently Deputy PM in the Chaudhry government). The shift of power Bavadra's election caused was undoubtedly a significant factor in the 1987 coups. And though represented as a united 'Fijian' action, the ensuing general chaos, and with their 'common adversary', the Indians, sidelined for the time being, the fighting over who would wield power actually gave a new lease of life to the old factional rivalries between the confederacies, and in particular between west and east.

Indians are relatively far more numerous in the west, and inter-ethnic intolerance has generally been less in evidence. It is also a region in which there are many land-leases which have not been renewed, resulting in Indian families who have farmed the land for generations being evicted from the only homes they have ever known. But while this is understandably uppermost in Indian concerns, it is not the only matter of concern to indigenous Fijians. Grumbles about the fact that western Fiji earned the lion's share of Fiji's income, but received the crumbs from the table in its distribution, go back to the early days of independence, and became sharply focused during the 1977 elections. Following this, Ratu Osea Gavidi (who has been so much to the fore in reports of the recent events in western Fiji) formed the Western United Front. Since that time, they have mounted a strong push for the formation of a fourth confederacy, the *Yasayasa Vaka Ra*, carving off everything west of a line dividing Viti Levu in half. This received even greater impetus in the rivalries that followed the coups. The reasoning is that while they may not have the traditional powerful dynasties, such a confederacy would have such economic clout that they would have to be reckoned with. The west has the greatest concentration of tourism, sugarcane, mining, and the pine-forest industry, and the international airport is there. Of major foreign-income earning industries, only the garment industry is predominantly in Suva, and it may be the hardest to re-establish when normalcy returns, having already been effectively destroyed by the present situation.

Speight shows no concern about the danger of a west/east split, as we see him posturing each night for the eager media that inexplicably continue to pander to his paranoid delusions of grandeur and report his every inane utterance. In one interview he said, 'Why not? Australia has eight or nine States, doesn't it?', thus showing his ignorance not only of the number of Australian political divisions, but also of the difference between the secession of part of a united country, and the federation of previously separate States. In truth, it is also extremely doubtful if he actually understands much about the forces at work in Fiji. His grasp of Fiji's history is clearly pretty hazy — for example, to justify his use of force, he keeps reiterating that Britain took Fiji by the force of the gun, whereas in fact it refused the first offers of cession by a cartel of powerful chiefs, and accepted it very reluctantly, and peacefully, after the offer was again urgently pressed. But Speight has also been out of Fiji for much of the period since independence, and does not have direct experience of, and certainly no scholarly apprehension of, the various forces that have moulded current Fijian politics, either inter-ethnic or intra-Fijian.

Viewed simplistically, it might appear as though the western chiefs should line up behind Speight's rhetoric about Fijian rights. But in fact, they have stated that they oppose him strongly and are demanding a return to democratic government. The reason is that they will already lose an enormous amount, as a result of the economic isolation Fiji will undoubtedly suffer, whatever happens from now on. Their prosperity depends on social and political stability, and their prosperity is the key to a greater share in power.

Also, though on the face of it their history should lead them to share Speight's opposition to the Mara dynasty and its allies, their positions are radically different. Speight is one of an increasing group of economic 'chancers' in such developing countries, and the chaos following 1987 opened up undreamed-of possibilities for them. The structure and accountability the Chaudhry government was imposing were disastrous from their viewpoint, and also set in train legal forces that, if permitted to take their course, must spell Speight's doom. Intent on self-preservation, he obviously saw the half-baked plot of disaffected third-raters that was brewing, as his opportunity to circumvent that happening, and he took control of it.

Speight has piggy-backed on the racist, 'nationalistic' rhetoric Rabuka developed to provide a plausible rationale for his actions following his coup in 1987. He is quick on his feet and has refined and amended this to suit the occasion, and predictably he has attracted a certain amount of support from Fijians, including a number of chiefs whose understandable anxieties about the preservation of their identity and land rights were once more brought to the fore by the Chaudhry government's proposed land legislation. Given that, what is actually most interesting is that the level of support is far less than Rabuka was able to marshall playing on the same fears, and much of that is doubtless down to Speight's opposition to Ratu Mara and his refusal to acknowledge the authority of the Great Council, which Rabuka was at pains to elevate. But in actuality a strong traditional leadership is as inimical to Speight's self-seeking, anarchic agenda as is a democratically elected government. While he deceitfully tries to make a display of acknowledging the chiefs, in fact he has no use for them, and has shown that he will reject anything they say or do which does not fall in behind his personal agenda.

The western chiefs' ambition, on the other hand, is to walk taller in the halls of traditional leadership, rather than to attempt to pull that leadership down. They recognise that, despite growing resistance to, and increasingly marginal relevance of, Fiji's chiefly system, the momentum that tradition has in Fiji will still carry it well into the foreseeable future. It would be a mistake to see the western chiefs' stated opposition to Speight as noble support for a multicultural Fiji, or for democratic institutions per se. While they must certainly be dismayed at the dark economic times that will inevitably result from his actions, the threat implicit in their declaration of a separate confederacy is not aimed at Speight, upon whom it can have no immediate effect and who seemingly cannot understand, or does not care about, its long-term implications. Rather, they are seizing the opportunity to move into the next act of their own ongoing campaign, and are attempting to better position themselves for the unstable situation and renewed jockeying for power that will inevitably ensue when the shooting dies down. Their implicit threat is that, unless they do well in the resulting carve-up of power, they might actually secede, an action that would totally destabilise Fiji and bring its viability as a nation-state under threat. While Fiji's west may possibly be economically viable on its own, it is far less clear that the remainder of Fiji would be.

All of which shows that, as is the case in the Solomons, the mix of ethnic division, traditional rivalries and modern economic power is a highly explosive brew. There have always been many more agendas in play from day one than the simplistic depiction of events, mainly in racial terms, might lead one to believe. Indeed, though Speight continues to try to play the 'race' card, apart from individual acts of thuggery, the current conflict has moved past even the pretence of being an ethnic issue, and is now between the gang of kidnappers and the (indigenous) Fijian army.

Finally, a plea that observers not see the sickening instances of vandalism, looting and violence that have occurred and continue to occur in Fiji as indicative of indigenous Fijian bellicosity or even widespread hostility toward Indians. That these particular occurrences are only incidentally ethnic is shown by the fact that many rural Indians are taking refuge from these thugs, with Fijian villagers. These are the actions of the ever-present cruising sharks who move in for the kill at any signs of weakness and distress. We see similar instances in crises and conflicts worldwide. In this case, Indians have been offered up by Speight's wild inflammatory utterances as an acceptable target, and in the chaotic climate generated by his actions, law-enforcement agencies are unable, even in some cases unwilling, to protect them. The perpetrators of these actions are utterly contemptible, but sadly such creatures are always with

coup

us — it's just that happily, most of the time, in a climate of law and order, they have fewer opportunities to act so concertedly or on such a scale. It is in fact a tribute to the customary decency of the wider ethnic Fijian community, and the responsible behaviour of the majority of the police and military, that Fiji has not developed into a Sarajevo or Kosovo. I do not believe it ever will, despite having little confidence that a resolution of the crisis is near.

THE 'GHOSTLY SMELL' OF INDIAN COOLIES TOO STRONG FOR SPEIGHT

Victor Lal

In a cruel twist of irony, George Speight and his band of racist and criminal henchmen, are clamouring for freedom from their temporary prison on Nukulau Island, a popular picnic spot outside the capital Suva.

The island is, ironically, a former departure point to Fiji's sugar fields for Indian coolies, the ancestors of deposed Prime Minister Mahendra Pal Chaudhry and other Indo-Fijians, whom Speight removed from power at the point of a gun because they, according to him, 'smelled' differently from the native Fijians.

George Speight, like Sitiveni Rabuka before him, cut short the tortuous journey of Indo-Fijians from plantation to parliament for the second time in their history in Fiji. As Speight and his racist storm-troopers complain of ill-treatment on the island, the memories of the harsh indenture days linger on in the Indo-Fijian minds. As one Indian labourer, who arrived on Nukulau Island in 1911, recalled: 'When we arrived in Fiji we were herded into a punt like pigs and taken to Nukulau where we stayed for a fortnight. We were given rice full of worms and kept and fed like animals. Later we were separated into groups for various employers to choose who they wanted. We got to Navua and were given a three-legged pot, a large spoon, and some rice. We then went to Nakaulevu where we saw the sugar lines.'

Even the Indian indentured women, who began arriving in Fiji from 1879 onwards, did not escape the yoke of slavery. According to

Miss Hannah Dudley of the Fiji Methodist Mission: 'They arrive in this country timid, fearful women, not knowing where they are to be sent. They are allotted to plantations like so many dumb animals. If they do not perform their work satisfactorily they are struck or fined, or sent to goal. The life on the plantations alters their demeanour and even their very faces. Some look crushed and broken-hearted, others sullen, others hard and evil. I shall never forget the first time I saw indentured women when they were returning from their day's work. The look on those women's faces haunts me.'

One hundred and twenty-one years later, the ancestors of these coolies are still being hunted, terrorised, brutalised, and some Indo-Fijian women even reportedly raped in Speight's new Fiji for the Fijians. The only difference is that from 1879 to 1920, when the indenture system came to an end, the violence and brutality were meted out by the white planters.

Today, they are being meted out by their new Fijian masters, beginning with Sitiveni Rabuka's racist coups of 1987, which unleashed the racist Frankenstein — George Speight — who is a product of European and Fijian ancestry, the so-called 'Marginal Man' in Fijian society.

One can but only express pity at the frailty of yesterday's so-called Mr Strongman. The Indian coolies endured nearly half a century of harsh treatment on their way to the various plantations from Nukulau Island. The late Australian historian K.L. Gillion, in his study of Indians in Fiji, concluded that their history would show how they 'continued to adapt to the land to which their great grandparents came under such unhappy circumstances'. If they were not yet Fijians, they were certainly Fiji-Indians. For the Indo-Fijians, the coups of May 1987, and now the attempted coup of 2000, that ousted their representatives from Parliament have arrested their painful progress from Nukulau Island to Fiji's national Parliament.

Their history, however, will record that their own displacement from British India in 1879 prevented the dispossession of the Fijian in colonial Fiji following the Deed of Cession in 1874. Indeed, ironically, the indentured Indian was uprooted specifically to prevent the disintegration of the Fijian way of life.

In 1978, Dr Satendra Nandan, the poet/academic who was among those seized in Parliament on 14 May 1987, had reminded the nation: 'It is interesting to speculate if this peasant labourer had not come to Fiji at a critical time, not only the Fijian way of life but many island communities in the South Pacific would have been disrupted and perhaps permanently dislocated. The planters needed labour, the British government wanted economic viability for political stability, and it is anyone's guess what they would have done to achieve this. Thus the displacement of the Indian prevented the dispossession of the Fijian. This may be the lasting and most significant contribution of the peasants from India. Without this the Fijian might have lost much of his land, and more tragically, his self-respect.'

Earlier, I referred to George Speight as the 'Marginal Man' in Fiji society, a phrase borrowed from an article by Harry M. Chambers entitled 'The Marginal Man in Fiji Society: Cultural Advantage or Dilemma'. Chambers noted that a marginal man is a person of mixed cultural heritage, obtained by way of marriage or as a result of sexual relations between ancestors of different cultural heritage. The Marginal Man is sometimes classified as a 'half-caste'.

In Fiji society, he is called Part-European. Chambers noted that the greatest advantage of being a marginal man in Fiji is that one has insight into more than one culture, and has the opportunity of bringing out the best parts of each culture he is a part of and combining them to suit himself. He has more choice than most people have. Above all, a marginal man can also mix more easily with members of a culture altogether separate from the one he has the greatest insight into, because he understands more and, thus, is able to mix with people on their own terms.

In Speight's case, he has failed all the peoples of Fiji; his European ancestory for disregarding the rule of law and parliamentary democoracy; the Fijian ancestory for the way he treated the Great Council of Chiefs, and his fellow Indo-Fijians with his rabid racist pronouncements.

Unfortunately, if there is any community in Fiji that can truly claim to be Fijian constitutionally, it is the Indo-Fijians, for as Chambers has pointed out, in Fiji society, biological half-castes were present long before European contact, resulting from the high frequency of Melanesian–Polynesian and, especially, Tongan–Fijian interaction and intermarriage.

Above all, Speight's detention on Nukulau Island should remind him of John Donne's immortal words: 'No Man Is An Island'.

In conclusion, as George Speight and his men of terror and violence ponder their Waterloo on 'Nukultraz Island', it is to be sincerely hoped that they will, if and when they are finally released from Nukulau, carry with them the spirit of the Indian coolies before them, who went on to give us a Garden of Eden, and not a racist 'Satan's Paradise' which Speight and Associates have turned Fiji into in the 21st century.

THE RACE BANDWAGON

Sanjay Ramesh

1. The Race Bandwagon

Race is a crude fact of life in Fiji. But the recent hijacking of an elected government in Fiji has nothing to do with race. It has to do with factional and provincial warlords, who seized the opportunity to facilitate their agenda. Indigenous Fijians were unhappy with the Chaudhry government and in particular with ALTA, changes to constitution, mahogany, and the Land Use Commission. The discontent gave rise to the Taukei Movement in April and a number of similar movements thereafter. Landowners and chiefs denounced the government for acting contrary to the interest of indigenous Fijians and wanted the government dissolved and the 1997 Constitution abrogated. Whipping up antagonism against the government were opposition politicians as well as factions from within the government's own coalition. The bizarre but understandable configuration of political interest in Fiji saw a strong anti-government mobilisation with some 5000 strong protesters on 28 April in Suva and the number rising to 10,000 by 19 May. All this came at a time when the government was fighting hard to sell its policy to indigenous Fijian chiefs.

The 1997 Constitution became the centre of discussion as opposition groups lobbied for its abrogation. The President of Fiji, Ratu Sir Kamisese Mara, was presented with a petition to remove the Chaudhry government and rescind the 1997 Constitution. While all this was happening, rumours in early April surfaced that a group of soldiers was behind moves to topple the government in a May 1987-type coup. The Fiji Military Forces (FMF) denied that there were any such moves from within the army. However, the rumour proved true when George Speight and seven FMF officers from the First Meridian Squadron hijacked the elected government on 19 May.

In what was to be a short stint at removing the Chaudhry government it became a gruelling stalemate with the hijackers jumping from one demand to another. Unlike the 1987 coup, the May 2000 takeover is seriously bungled. Without a clear objective and direction, the rebel leader George Speight attacked and accused Indo-Fijians for all the social and economic ills plaguing indigenous Fijians. However, he further illustrated that Indo-Fijians were different in all respects from their indigenous Fijian counterparts and as a result they had to be removed entirely from the political scene. This was the initial Indo-Fijian bashing, which took a rather sinister form when Indo-Fijian residents of Muanirewa were attacked by bandits loyal to George Speight, who argued that Indo-Fijians controlled the economy and lived in style and luxury while indigenous Fijians lived in abject poverty. Once again the focus was on the business community in Fiji.

Most of the shops in the towns and cities across Fiji are owned by *Gujaratis* whereas descendants of indentured labourers are still on the farm or part of the growing Indo-Fijian middle class. Some have acquired fame and fortune while others have gone into business. Compared with the *Gujaratis*, descendants of indentured labourers own less than 20 per cent of businesses in Fiji. Shopping strips in all major towns and cities are predominantly *Gujarati* and hence the myth that Indo-Fijians own businesses and have a lot of wealth.

Whilst Indo-Fijians perform better in education, commerce and agriculture, indigenous Fijians are not far behind. Educated indigenous Fijians are also part of a growing middle class while a large number of Fijian families, mostly from the islands, continue to struggle in the urban slums of Suva. A lack of proper housing, compulsory education measures and some form of national employment service breed violent and disillusioned indigenous Fijian youths, who take on a profession of crime at an early age.

All this points to a system that is strongly elitist. Under the 1990 Constitution, cronies of the SVT party amassed huge wealth and privilege under the guise of 'Fijian political paramountcy'. Under the 1997 Constitution much of the elitist centralised system remained and the indigenous, grassroots Fijian never understood what the Constitution provided for them. When the Chaudhry government released Bills 15 and 16 to amend the Native Land Trust Board (NLTB) Act, the opposition cried foul and demanded an immediate repeal. In fact, under the proposed law, future legislation governing Crown Schedule A and B would not go before the NLTB. Instead, the Cabinet reserved the authority to recommend changes to the President of Fiji. The intention was that Crown Schedule A and B would eventually revert back to the original indigenous Fijian landowners. Apart from that, changes to Section 194 of the Constitution allowed indigenous Fijian Members to continue holding both political and traditional offices. Under the 1997 Constitution, the *Bose Levu Vakaturaga* or Great Council of Chiefs, Fijian Affairs Board, *Bose ni Yasana* (Head of the Provincial Council) and *Bose ni Tikiai* (Head of the District Council) were deemed public offices.

The Deputy Prime Minister of Fiji, Adi Kuini Speed, made it absolutely clear that on amendments to NLTB Act, a sub-committee would be established and views of all affected parties sought. However, by then, the SVT mounted a massive disinformation campaign which largely downplayed the entrenched constitutional safeguards for all indigenous Fijian institutions. Under Section 185 (1) of the 1997 Constitution, the following indigenous Fijian institutions are fully protected:

(a) Fijian Affairs Act;
(b) Fijian Development Fund Act;
(c) Native Lands Act;
(d) Native Land Trust Act;
(e) Rotuma Act; Rotuman Lands Act;
(g) Banaban Lands Act; or
(h) Banaban Settlement Act; including a Bill prepared in consequence of the enactment of this Constitution:

All Bills regarding the above are deemed not to have been passed by the Senate unless at its third reading in that House, it is supported by the votes of at least 9 of the 14 members of the Senate appointed by the *Bose Levu Vakataturaga.*

Disinformation continues to play a large part in Fiji today. The hijackers' claim that an Indo-Fijian Prime Minister can single-handedly dismantle an entrenched indigenous Fijian institution does not hold up to scrutiny. It confirms that race has been used to facilitate sectional provincial interest under the guise of "Fijian political paramountcy".

However, all the half-baked effort of George Speight will amount to zero if constructive programs to lift the overall standard of disaffected indigenous Fijians are not put in place. There has to be a number of initiatives put in place straight away. These include a Fijian business institute, compulsory education, rural development and creation of a viable communal-based village economy. This will arrest unskilled and uneducated Fijian youths from migrating to the cities. A good start will be to establish an office of Indigenous Fijian Improvement with qualified and skilled policy specialists. This office shall advise the Interim Government on specific measures and programs. Once implemented, the programs have to be evaluated against stringent performance criteria. All of these cannot materialise without the support of Indo-Fijians, who must be included in any Interim Government of Fiji. By right, they should constitute 40 per cent of the total number of Ministers.

If the above is not done soon, a majority of indigenous Fijians will unlikely see any changes to their economic life even in this century. Finally, George Speight and his group have no credibility whatsoever when it comes to fighting for indigenous Fijian rights and the abrogation of the 1997 Constitution — agreed by SVT, FAP and GCC — is a grave error on the part of the military.

If for any reasons indigenous Fijians were unhappy with the Chaudhry government, then they certainly should have waited and voted as a bloc and defeated Chaudhry in the general elections of 2004. A group of people with guns cannot determine constitution, order and government in any society, let alone Fiji. It is therefore imperative that the hijackers are condemned by all Fijians.

2. Militarisation of Fijian Nationalism

The recent hijacking of an elected government by sectional interests in Fiji does not come as a surprise, since plans have been in progress for a year to undermine Prime Minister Mahendra Chaudhry, who seemingly fell out of favour with Fiji's elite powerbrokers.

Debate continued for nearly a year on the results of the May 1999 general election. Starting with Rabuka's post-election outbursts, many indigenous Fijians believed that Indo-Fijians en masse rejected the Rabuka–Reddy compromise and voted as a bloc to install the Chaudhry government. However, behind this assertion lies a deeper, more culturally based explanation for Indo-Fijian action. The vote against Rabuka and Reddy was not against the constitutional compromise but against Rabuka, who continues to be seen as an individual responsible for executing the coups and causing enormous pain and suffering to Indo-Fijians.

No doubt that had Reddy formed a partnership with someone other than Rabuka, he and his party would not have been punished so severely at the polls. Things went from bad to worse with the about-turn of SVT under the leadership of Ratu Inoke Kubuabola — one of the leaders who carried out the destabilisation campaign against the Bavadra government. Joining him were other disgruntled politicians, including Ratu Timoci Silatolu and Ratu Tu'akitau of the Fijian Association Party, Mitieli Bulanauca of the Christian Democratic Alliance (VLV), Fijian Nationalist Viliame Savu and former members of the Party of National Unity led by Apisai Tora — not to mention reported meetings between a dubious Iranian-born Swedish arms dealer and members of the opposition and the army on 6 May in Colo-i-Suva.

It all points to institutional fragility that characterises many multi-ethnic states. All the way from the Balkans to Africa, self-styled military warlords and thugs have assumed ethnic leadership and waged cultural persecution of other ethnic groups. In the case of Fiji, indigenous Fijians were extended a franchise in 1963 and since then have engaged in communal voting. The shift towards common voting among largely urban indigenous Fijians resulted in the Bavadra government, which was deposed in the coups of 1987. The process of developing any meaningful culture of democracy among indigenous Fijians was thwarted in 1987 and then given a knee-jerk start in 1997 with the promulgation of the new compromise constitution. At that time, SVT Cabinet Ministers remained steadfast in their defiance for any concessions to Indo-Fijians and all this is very well reflected in the SVT submission in October 1995 to the Constitution Review Commission.

Indigenous Fijian political paramountcy remains a powerful ideological tool. This paramountcy is based on the Deed of Cession of 1874 and the concept that the government of Fiji shall remain under the hegemony of the *Taukei* or indigenous Fijians and that *vulagi* or foreigners have to participate in the national political economy of Fiji on indigenous Fijian terms. While all this sounds very good, the problem still remains of indigenous Fijian disunity, which played a large part in compromising SVT's political position in the last general election. Rabuka in his biography pointed out that provincialism was eating away the cultural fabric of Fijian society. However, for the moment this green–eyed monster is conveniently in the background while the Indian bogey remains of urgent concern. In the case of contemporary Fiji, this paragraph from Dr Frank Harvey is most telling:. 'Ethnic identities are evoked in certain structural circumstances to advance the material and political interests of actors whose primary purposes are not ethnic. Subsequent myth making and the dredging up of past events become symbols around which ethnic groups coalesce. These symbols make inter-ethnic violence appear just, honorable and legitimate.'

It means that those whipping up the chimera of Indian dominance in Fiji are doing so to fan fears of cultural insecurity, which is endemic among grassroots indigenous Fijians. Agitators like Apisai Tora have called for Indo-Fijians to be repatriated. A similar call was made by the late Sakeasi Butadroka in 1975. Tora's own political record is anything but consistent. After being in Alliance stalwart, Tora became a leading figure in the 1987 Taukei Movement and was a Minister in the Interim Government until he had his share of fall-out with Mara. In 1992, he formed the multicultural All National Congress (ANC), which was disbanded in 1995 following a merger between the Fijian Association and the ANC. In 1998, Tora spearheaded the Party of National Unity (PANU) as an opposition party to the SVT and joined hands with the Fijian Association and the Fiji Labour Party later in that year.

After losing his seat, Tora became bitter and hostile and blamed Indo-Fijian voters for thwarting his political ambition. After going public with his comments, Apisai Tora started his own secret project and resigned from PANU. Prime Minister Mahendra Chaudhry who was previously seen as committed to multiculturalism became a dictatorial monster, harbouring secret ambitions to dismember current Fijian land ownership. For Tora, Chaudhry had to be stopped in his tracks before he undermined 'Fijian culture'. It was shocking to see a non-indigenous Fijian sitting with the high chiefs at the Great Council of Chiefs. Not only that but the Land Use Commission, ALTA, recent charges to the Constitution, the mahogany deal, provincial council funding, and civil service reforms were seen as not in the best interest of Fijians. Capitalising on certain concerns, Tora and his gang launched the Taukei Movement in April.

After a failed Taukei Movement protest march on 20 April, organisers went back to the drawing board and promised a better performance for the march in Suva on 28 April. About 4000 people marched through Suva in support of the SVT party and the Taukei Movement for the Prime Minister to step down. A group of SVT and Taukei Movement members later presented their petition to the Boselevu Vakaturaga, or the Great Council of Chiefs. The petition called for the dissolution of the Chaudhry government, changes to the constitution, the proposed Land Use Commission to be abolished, all Schedule A and B land to be returned to landowners and the mahogany deal to be reviewed. Participating in the march were members of the Fijian Association Party and the Christian Democrats. Another protest march was held by the Nationalist Vanua Tako Lavo Party on 19 May. By then certain commercial interests had thrown support behind the destabilisation campaign. It was rumoured that a group within the 15,000 protestors would start riots in Suva on 19 May. However, unfortunately, the looting and burning of mainly Indo-Fijian businesses went out of control.

Following an intensification of anti-government activities, moves were afoot from within the Coalition government to move a motion of no confidence against Prime Minister Chaudhry. It is believed that Dr Tupeni Baba, who is rumoured to have supported the nationalist protest on 19 May, was to be installed as the new Prime Minister of Fiji. However, that was not to happen because George Speight and his six gun men had other plans.

George Speight, a failed businessman and a recognised fraud from Tailevu, along with six members of the Counter Revolutionary Warfare Unit, stormed Parliament and held government MPs, including the Prime Minister, at gunpoint. Speight, who has no notable history of championing indigenous Fijian rights, had appeared in Suva Magistrates Court on a foreign exchange scam and has dubious links to various pyramid schemes in Australia. In fact Speight saw his fortune quickly evaporate with the victory of the Coalition government. Among other things, Speight was removed as the Chairman of the Fiji Hardwood Corporation and was fired by Health Insurance Fiji Limited. Despite these setbacks, Speight was a major player in the mahogany deal with the US-based Timber Resource Management (TRM). When it was certain that the Coalition government would give the lucrative multi-million dollar timber contract to the British-based Commonwealth Development Corporation (CDC), Speight and his group started advising landowners that they had a better deal with the TRM.

Immediately following a campaign of disinformation, chiefs and landowners started to criticise the government, which referred the matter to the Great Council of Chiefs at its 26–28 April meeting at Raffles Tradewinds Hotel in Suva. Apart from lobbying against the government, Speight and his group, mainly from the SVT party, conspired with an arms dealer to illegally import automatic weapons into Fiji. The plan was hatched with the assistance of certain businesses to bring in arms and ammunition via Vanua Levu. Army officers were recruited to provide direction and support for the whole operation. While the planning and execution went on with precision, certain chiefs of the Kubuna confederacy were informed and their support assured just in case anything went wrong.

The plan was to hijack the government, abrogate the 1997 Constitution, remove the President, and install a Taukei government under the leadership of one of the Kubuna chiefs. The hostages were to be held for a week with anticipation that the overall disgust with the Chaudhry government would lead to an outright indigenous Fijian support of George Speight and his men. However, unfortunately, things did not go as planned. The Great Council of Chiefs gave unanimous support to Mara to resolve the crisis as some Kubura chiefs found themselves siding with the terrorists. Mara refused to accept George Speight's Taukei government, but gave in to his demands by dismissing the Coalition government.

With the President holding firm, Speight let out his thugs to provoke the military and the police. As a result, two soldiers and a journalist were wounded and a policeman from the west killed. After intense negotiations between the army and the President, Mara stepped aside on 29 May as the military imposed its rule on Fiji and repealed the 1997 Constitution. However, talks between the army and George Speight went nowhere as Speight imposed one new demand after another.

In the end, institutional fragility followed by a serious underdeveloped democratic culture, mainly among indigenous Fijians, allowed radical elements to manipulate the grassroots by creating a myth of a non-existent threat to land and identity. Indigenous Fijians have only their leadership to blame for their economic backwardness. The only outcome of a twelve-year experiment to transform indigenous Fijians into successful businessmen is disillusionment, failure, militancy and George Speight.

THE STRANGE SAGA OF SPEIGHT'S SIEGE IN SUVA

Graeme Dobell

Fiji's media were rare institutional winners out of the strange saga of Speight's siege in Suva. Fiji's journalists were one of the few groups to gain stature during the 56 days that George Speight held MPs hostage in the Parliament compound.

The role Fiji's journalists were able to play in 2000 is a significant contrast to the two military coups of 1987, when they were closed down or muzzled. The professionalism of Fiji's media during the long period of intense pressure caused by Speight's siege was a high point in the often-sorry tale of South Pacific journalism. And it washed away some of the bitter taste lingering from the abuse of Fiji's media 13 years earlier.

When Sitiveni Rabuka took power in 1987, the army closed down newspapers and a military censor controlled the news broadcast by Radio Fiji. One of the few light moments of the heavy-handed censorship regime came when Commonwealth leaders ejected Fiji from the Commonwealth. That news came through early in the morning and the army officer on duty couldn't raise any of his superiors to get a ruling on how the information should be broadcast. He thus refused to approve or reject any copy on the Commonwealth decision. The editors preparing Radio Fiji's main morning bulletin came up with a solution, which did not directly break censorship guidelines. They took a direct feed of the hourly bulletin broadcast from Melbourne by Radio Australia. So, the news that Fiji had been cast out of the Commonwealth was preceded by the ABC news theme and conveyed by an Australian reporter. It symbolised the helpless state imposed on Fiji's media.

In the 2000 crisis, by contrast, there was no censorship for the domestic media and no attempt by the Ministry of Information to control international reporting. This time, Fiji was served by three newspapers (*The Fiji Times, The Post* and *The Sun*), two radio networks (Radio Fiji and FM 96) and the television service, Fiji One. This time the internet was a factor, influencing both international and national agendas. (George Speight, inside the Parliament compound, could log on to the web to check how he was being covered.) This time, Fiji's reporters were able to keep working. The rumours sweeping Fiji had to compete with real news. The international reporters too, did a better job because they were working from a solid basis of information provided by Fiji's media.

Each of Fiji's media outlets made inevitable mistakes in reporting a prolonged crisis produced by deep ethnic and political forces. But the overall coverage gave Fijians timely and accurate information. Other key institutions — the Parliament, the army, police, Fiji's legal system and the Great Council of Chiefs — were notable for how they stuttered or failed in dealing with the crisis.

George Speight produced more than a terrorist siege. There were Pacific rhythms at work and political interests at play. The voice Speight projected, via the media, illustrated a leadership and institutional paralysis. Elements in the army, police and the chiefly structure were backing Speight overtly or covertly. And Fiji's media gave Fijians much of the news needed to interpret these forces.

The Prelude

The May edition of Fiji's monthly magazine, *The Review*, was published in late April, more than three weeks before Speight's group seized the Parliament on 19 May. *The Review* marked its eighth birthday with the cover headline 'Operation Chaos', and an illustration of a 'To Do List':

1. Shut down all essential services
2. Mobilise protest marchers
3. Remove Mahendra Chaudhry as PM
4. Restore Fijian leadership
5. Control Fiji

The article by deputy editor Tamarisi Digitaki anticipated a legal campaign of civil disobedience waged by the Fiji nationalist Taukei Movement to topple the Chaudhry government elected in May 1999. The cover story (like Mahendra Chaudhry himself) downplayed the idea of violent action because the army was proclaiming its loyalty: 'Another military coup seems an unlikely option at this stage. [Military chief] Commodore Frank Bainimarama has already denounced allegations of the army's involvement. In fact, the army personnel whom *The Review* talked to agree that if there is another coup, then blood, and lots of it, will be shed this time. That alone makes it a very unattractive option. On the other hand, it shouldn't be forgotten that no one thought military intervention was possible in 1987.'

The key factor in the scenario painted by *The Review* was the real threat of violence. The article did not directly anticipate the split in the military, with Parliament seized by the army's specialist force, the Counter Revolutionary Warfare Unit. But Tamarisi Digitaki accurately caught the jittery mood in Suva because of 'the similarities between the events leading up to Rabuka's first coup in 1987 and the current situation. Political unrest prevails now as it did back then and political correctness aside, more and more Fijians are resenting the fact that an Indian is in power.'

The judgement of Australia's top diplomat in Suva, Sue Boyd, was that unease was so widespread, Chaudhry was only days away from being overthrown by his own MPs when Speight struck. Australia's High Commissioner told the ABC: 'What is actually ironic is that our friends in the Fiji Labour Party told us that they themselves had decided that Mahendra Chaudhry had to go.' Boyd said the Party planned to replace Chaudhry with his deputy, Tupeni Baba, an indigenous Fijian. Others in Suva were sceptical that the party room revolt would have disposed of Chaudhry. The Prime Minister had previously overcome his colleagues' questions and doubts. In the words of one Suva journalist: 'Mahendra was always the strongest one there. He would have just stared them down again and they would have shut up.'

Chaudhry's treatment of Fiji's media was sometimes as brutal as his treatment of his own MPs. Soon after being elected Prime Minister he attacked the *Fiji Times* for ts 'distorted and doctored news'. The international journalists' group Reporters Without Borders, commented that Chaudhry was irritated by the paper's close ties with the former Prime Minister, Sitiveni Rabuka. Chaudhry accused the *Fiji Times* of encouraging 'subversive actions and provoking racism and sedition'. In November 1999, the Chaudhry government announced a proposal to set up a media court to enforce professional standards and punish offenders. The Pacific Islands News Association responded virulently: 'Mahendra Chaudhry will become the first civilian dictator of a South Pacific Island if he maintains his threat to legislate against press freedom.' Fiji's political and media climate was becoming febrile.

The Drama

The US 'gonzo' journalist, Hunter S. Thompson, once observed: 'When the going gets weird, the weird turn professional.' During the Speight siege, there was a lot of weirdness in evidence, and it seemed to infect many of those who should have been giving professional service. To illustrate the roller coaster ride, I offer scenes from three consecutive days. In their cumulative effect, they were both dramatic and bizarre.

It is Saturday, 27 May, just over a week after the seizure of the Parliament on Friday, 19 May. During the previous week the Great Council of Chiefs has met, called for the release of the hostages and backed the President, Ratu Sir Kamisese Mara. George Speight — the self-proclaimed champion of indigenous rights and traditional power — has told Fiji's highest traditional body he will not accept their chiefly order or obey Ratu Mara.

The police, saying they can't maintain order, have handed over to the army, which has set up control points around the Parliament. On Saturday morning the first gun battle occurs. A mob of Speight supporters clash with army troops near the front entrance of Parliament. Army soldiers fire volleys of shots into the ground sending people screaming in all directions. Two soldiers and a TV cameraman are wounded.

In the afternoon we go from gunfights to Government House. Ratu Mara calls reporters to his official mansion overlooking the bay, only a few kilometres from the Parliament. The President announces that he has dismissed the Chaudhry government because it can no longer perform its duties. He will take executive power and seek to resolve the crisis. Mahendra Chaudhry may not be able to return to office, even after he is freed.

The next day, Sunday, 28 May, after church, more than a thousand Fijians — all in their best outfits, clutching their Bibles — visit Parliament for what amounts to a celebration, a revival service of singing and speeches praising indigenous rights. It's a beautiful day and the singing, clapping, dancing and preaching take place in the parking area of the Parliament, in sight of the chamber where the Fijian MPs are held, backing onto the Ministerial offices where the Indian MPs are held separately. One of the gospel songs has as its chorus the line, 'I don't care what people say, what the world may say or do'. It is an apt line for a Fiji which is turning inward. There are several layers of irony in this joyous expression of Christianity and Fijian identity. The reverse side, the dark side, comes later the same day in the evening, when a mob of about 200 Speight supporters come rampaging out of Parliament to attack Fiji's television station. Fiji One's Sunday night current affairs program, Close-up, has carried some less than complimentary observations about Speight. The mob crash into the studio. Fifteen minutes after the mob, I find the front door locked but all its glass smashed out. Every piece of glass in the offices and studio has been shattered. It truly looks like a bomb has exploded, but there is no sign of blast marks or smoke. It is an amazing feat of ingenuity and dedication that the station is back broadcasting within a matter of days. In a confrontation a couple of hundred metres away a policeman is shot several times and murdered. The first shooting death.

On Monday 29 May, Fiji is in shock. The weekend toll is one policeman murdered, two Fijian soldiers wounded and one TV cameraman wounded. A full military curfew is announced. That night, after the 8pm curfew, the military escorts the domestic and international media out to the Queen Elizabeth Barracks. The military commander, Frank Bainimarama, announces that Ratu Mara is gone. The military leadership has gone to the President and told him that he is not up to the task. They don't think he can resolve the crisis, and for his own safety he should head back to his home island. The military has taken over. We are back to the future — back to 1987. So in a week and a half Mahendra Chaudhry is overthrown three times ... by Speight, by Mara and then by the military.

At this point the siege was less than a quarter way through its eventual course. Yet Fiji was already past its point of no return. Speight's original outrage was compounded and expanded by significant Fijian institutions, and by flashes of violence and lawlessness that ran throughout the saga. The longer the crisis ran, the more it became clear this was a fight between indigenous Fijians. Along with the carnage inflicted on the economy, the greatest damage was done to indigenous Fijian institutions. In 1987, the prestige of the Great Council of Chiefs and the army — as expressions of Fijian power — was enhanced. This time, George Speight opened splits in the Fijian community, exposing tensions between regions, rivalry amongst the chiefs and the confused loyalties of the army. By removing Mara, the army opened a complicated struggle among the chiefs about future traditional leadership. This time, Fijians could not really pretend they were struggling solely with Indo-Fijians. Really, they were struggling with each other. In Speight's daily press conferences, his attack increasing y turned from Indo-Fijians to the failings of Fijian leadership. The version offered by Speight was that Fijian leaders had helped the spread of Western ideas of democracy, which eroded the rights and power of indigenous F jians. Here is one example of Speight's musings to the media, from week six of the siege:

You know it's a problem of leadership, more than anything else really. This country has been in Fijian leadership for 29 of the last 30 years. And that's 29 of the last 30 years of so-called emergence into the 21st century. It's been in Fijian hands, our leadership. Mahendra Chaudhry just came in the last five minutes, but he certainly didn't help by what he did. So, Fijian leadership over the last 29 years, and I speak specifically of his former excellency Ratu Sir Kamisese Mara and Sitiveri Rabuka; they pursued a style of leadership that did nothing but perpetuate the philosophies and social attitudes that the English left us in 1970, when we became independent, after 96 years, almost a century of British rule in this country. And I dare say they should have taken the opportunity then to do what I'm doing now in the year 2000. It's almost 30 years too late. But that's my point precisely. Better 30 years too late than not at all.

George Speight used Rabuka's old coup script and expected the army to play its 1987 role, to fall in behind the coup. Speight's whole approach was predicated on the army legitimising the seizure of Parliament. In the end, the army endorsed the overthrow of Chaudhry, but would not directly embrace Speight. Thus, Speight sat and waited to see what would turn up. He became emboldened by the weakness of the institutional responses and the media attention. In the end Speight made the mistake of believing his own publicity, and overplayed his hand after the hostages were released.

Speight was selected as the rebel figurehead because of his media skills. He quickly became a face known around the world because of his daily press conferences. So the domestic and international media were weapons in the political struggle waged from behind the parliamentary gates. The *Fiji Times* made an important point about the rebel media strategy midway through the siege, when it stopped referring to Speight as the coup leader but as the coup spokesman. The *Fiji Times* editor, Netani Rika, said Speight was chosen by those organising the coup attempt because he knew how to articulate the message in ways useful to print, radio and TV: 'I'd say the best call we made was to stop calling George Speight the coup leader when it became obvious that he wasn't. And I think that started the move towards finding out exactly who the mystery person or people were behind this whole charade.'

During the weeks of standoff, it became clear that in negotiations with the military Speight had to refer to others for approval. Inside the compound, a veto was held by the former special forces commander, Ilisoni Ligairi. Outside the compound, chiefly backers emerged, plus important players such as the former head of intelligence, Colonel Metuisela Mua, who had been dismissed by Mahendra Chaudhry. Less constrained in some areas than the Fiji media, foreign reporters were sometimes able to provide important profiles of such figures from the shadows of the coup.

The free access of the media in and out of the Parliament compound virtually throughout the siege was an extraordinary experience. Partly, the access was possible because this was not just a terrorist crime. It was also part of a political process. The military regime proclaimed an exclusion zone around the Parliament but it was never enforced for the media until the last few hours before Mahendra Chaudhry was released.

The international media contingent covering the coup came mainly from Australia and New Zealand. At the height of the story there were more than 100 reporters, cameapeople, producers and tape editors in Suva. Almost all stayed at the one hotel, the Centra. One or two phone calls to the Centra were all that was needed to get the international contingent for a press conference in Parliament or at military headquarters, the Queen Elizabeth Barracks. Speight was a ready performer, providing hundreds of interviews at news conferences, via the phone and in 'simsats' for the TV cameras. The word simsat stands for a 'simulated satellite interview'. A crew would go into Parliament equipped with TV gear and a mobile phone. The interviewer in Sydney, London or Atlanta would talk to Speight who would hear the questions via an earpiece in the mobile phone. Speight's answers were then sent by satellite to home base where they were intercut with vision of the interviewer's questions to produce the interview.

To travel to the siege involved a short journey through a number of military roadblocks. A reporter would leave the Centra, turn right and drive 300 metres to the first checkpoint. After being waved through, the drive went past Government House on the left and the harbour on the right. After a further kilometre, there was another slowdown to pass through the next army checkpoint. Go another kilometre, turn left up the hill and enter via the rear entrance of Parliament. Each visit meant handing over a licence ID or pass with a photo (in my case, the pass I use to get access to the press gallery in the Australian Parliament). Equipment was searched, names listed, and then media were waved in to the assembly area where Speight held his regular press conferences. Usually, the only areas reporters could not visit were the chamber and executive offices where the hostages were held.

To answer Speight's media profile, the military regime, in seizing power, had to create its own face. The military had to fight a rolling stream of Speight interviews and pronouncements. The chief spokesman used in this role was Lieutenant Colonel Filipo Tarakinikini, who eventually achieved an international media profile close to that of Speight. Tarakinikini was a coolly professional voice for the military in answering Speight (an ironic role because of persistent questions about how much knowledge Tarakinikini had of the plans to seize Parliament).

Tarakinikini said the military regime's media policy was not to gag reporters but to counter Speight by telling the truth; 'The tug of war was based on the fact that we knew what he was trying to sell to the people was not true, was not credible, and was not going to hold up in time. The challenge was for us to ensure that we get to the people and get them to believe that what we stood for was the truth ... What George Speight was coming up with was racist, was discriminatory, was against our principles and was not going to work for them.'

Q: Why did the military not do what it did in 1987? Why did you not close down the newspapers, impose censorship and put military officers in the radio stations to control what was broadcast? Why did you do it differently this time?

Tarakinikini: Because we did not believe in it. We did not believe that the way it was done in 1987 was correct. There was nothing to be gained from gagging the media. And the media is now a powerful force in the world and we had to get the media on side. Without the media then our message couldn't get out to people and to the world.

Q: What lessons did you draw from the 1987 experience?

Tarakinikini: I'm not privy to the reasoning of the decision makers in 1987 but certainly this time round we had learned from 1987. The stance the military took from day one is that we were not going to lie to our own people. We were going to tell them the truth. We were not going to sweep anything under the carpet.

The commitment to truth was partly a response to the range of media outlets within Fiji (which could, in theory, have been censored), but also internet sites which could not be controlled. The military spokesman said many of the web sites outside Fiji were being fed information from Fiji. 'Generally the media handled the situation quite well,' Tarakinikini said. 'What was disturbing was the web sites on the internet that were publishing a lot of information based on rumours and which was being accessed by a sizable number of Fiji watchers outside Fiji in the international community. This is where we could not censor anything and it was quite disturbing the amount of damage that was done by the internet sites.'

In the 1987 coups, Fiji did not have television. By 2000, villagers were used to seeing their own TV news and also TV news services from New Zealand, Australia and the British BBC.

The editor of the *Fiji Times*, Netani Rika, reflected on the media awareness found even among villagers who staged land occupations or blocked roads: 'People know just how powerful the media is when it comes to putting your message across. That was reflected in how both the security forces and the rebel got their message across, not only here but overseas. There were even times when smaller rebel groups around the country refused to talk to the local journalists, saying "We want to see the BBC people. We'll only talk to the BBC people". It was only when the foreign TV crews came onto the scene that they would speak both to the foreign crews and then to the local journalists.'

Q: So there was an element of media management even out on the blockades. When villagers threw up their roadblocks?

Netani Rika: Yes, while it was frustrating for our staff at times that these people didn't want us at first, it did provide an element of humour in otherwise trying times.

Q: Do you think there is a greater respect for journalism and what journalism can do for Fiji? Or was it merely a pragmatic judgement that it is harder now to control the various media outlets? Was it principle or pragmatism?

Netani Rika: I think it was pragmatism. These guys had to get their message across. They had to use the media to do it. They had to state what they were fighting for in the case of the rebels. In the case of the military they had to show the public they were in control so they made practical use of the media.

Acting on the time-honoured journalistic principle that reporters catch and kill their own, some of the strongest criticism of the performance of the 'international hacks' came from within the ranks in the Centra. The experienced South Pacific correspondent for Agence France-Presse, Michael Field, wrote a couple of features on the press corps. One, republished in the local papers, ended with an ironic comment on the foreign reporters rushing sheep-like after each other: 'If you really want to bug the international media, get a camera and notebook and run like hell through the lobby of the Centra. Dozens of reporters and cameramen will run after you — because you will look as if you know what the next story is. We of the international media don't have a clue.'

In a piece headed 'Farewell to coup coup land' after Chaudhry was released, Michael Field pondered how the media used and were used by the rebels: 'Obviously George Speight was something of a ringmaster at this game, and for a time he became our monster, our property. He could whistle us up to Parliament in a shot and we'd be there, listening to his endless raves. He would try, too, to engage reporters in friendly banter — but fortunately most of us resisted the idea of backslapping and laughing with a man holding a gun at others.'

CHAUDHRY'S LAST PUBLIC ADDRESS BEFORE HE WAS MADE HOSTAGE

Mahendra Chaudhry

Two days before his government was taken over by George Speight and group, Prime Minister Mahendra Chaudhry spoke to about 500 people at a public meeting in Nasinu. That was probably his last public utterance before he was made hostage — shut behind parliament doors till now. What he said at the public meeting at Nasole Temple on Wednesday 17 May is very much today a concern for everyone — racial unity. He said the government's latest priority was to work out strategies to unite the nation. 'Fiji is the only home and hope of all people living here — we must have a common goal and hope,' he said. He also said that indigenous Fijians and Rotumans should know that their rights and interests take precedence over the rights and interests of other communities, should there be a conflict of interest between Fijians and other communities.

We are completing our first year in Parliament, this coming Friday the 19th of May. Actually, I should have been here earlier than this evening to meet with you and share our views. But it is better late than never.

I have been trying to persuade my Members of Parliament in your constituency to convene meetings regularly, particularly when Parliament is sitting every second month and when we have other Members of Parliament from other parts of the country in Suva, so that we can go around and meet with the people, in and around Suva, in Nasinu, Nausori, Lami, because there are all of us here for two or three weeks at a time every second month.

But for some reason it has not been possible before now to arrange such a meeting. Having taken the initiative now, I hope that your MPs here will try and hold meetings in different parts of their constituency at more regular intervals.

Tonight you will want to hear, as you have already heard from two of my Ministers and the Honourable Krishna Dutt, as to what the government has done since taking office some 12 months ago. As you know if you have read our manifesto, and this was widely distributed, you would have found that we have highlighted the problems we faced as a nation last year. We laid out this problem and then alongside that we said what we are going to do about these problems if we were elected.

And as a government we had told you that our top priority would be poverty alleviation: that we will work and give priority to those programs and we will allocate resources to those programs which will help the poor because they come first. And we have begun doing this. In fact we began doing this within the first and second month after assuming office.

We have said that we will bring down food prices on basic items by removing VAT and customs duty. We have done that. When we did that, there was a lot of hue and cry from the people. There were claims that the government was going to become bankrupt because they are giving away so much money by removing VAT and duty on these items. But this has not happened. Government revenue is very buoyant.

You would have read this morning's paper, the *Daily Post*, on the front page that the government is bringing 17 more basic consumer items under price control. And these are items that every family uses every day in their homes. And after a survey was done in 1998, it was the recommendation of those who conducted the survey, government officials, that these items should be brought under price control. But the previous government did not want to do it. We have done that and we hope that by putting these 17 items under price control there will be further reductions in living costs.

For the poor, the disabled and the disadvantaged with no income and no means of support, the government in its 2000 budget increased the family assistance allowance by $1.5 million. So there is now $6.5 million a year for what used to be called the Destitute Allowance. We call it Family Assistance Allowance. That is the second initiative we took.

We promised the poor that we would help you when we are elected. There are many people who are poor, who live in rural areas and in and around cities and towns. There is urban poverty also. We are very familiar with the living conditions of many people out in your area, in squatter settlements and elsewhere who live in those conditions because they cannot earn enough income and support their families and live a life of dignity. So we moved to do that

The Minister of Works has already told you that we have already knocked down the charges for electricity and further reductions in these charges will take place soon. For those with incomes of $6500 a year and less we have promised we will bring down the Housing Authority interest rates from 11.5 per cent to 6 per cent. We have done that. It couldn't be done overnight but we have done that within the year.

And for those of you who are earning more than $6500 and are borrowers from the Housing Authority we will soon reduce the rate from 11.5 per cent progressively and it will come down. So that is another promise that we have fulfilled. We said to you that we will re-establish students loans scheme for children of poor families or those families with inadequate incomes who wanted to send their children to tertiary institutions like USP, FIT etc. but who could not do so because they do not have enough income to pay the fees or they couldn't get a scholarship. We said the government would provide the money under a scheme known as the Children's Loan Scheme. We have done that. From this year we have established a Children's Loan Scheme to assist children and poor families access a tertiary education and we have provided $1 million this year. This may go up as resources permit. So that is another promise that we have fulfilled.

We said we would promote development in rural areas by allocating more money and resources for agriculture. My Minister for Agriculture has already spoken about that. And there is a very good reason for doing that. Every country should produce enough food to feed the population. Food security is very important. We cannot rely on imported food. That is the wrong strategy.

We must produce as much food as we can within the country so that food is cheap and import only food that we cannot grow locally. And for that if we have to protect our farmers we should protect them. That is why we helped to revive Rewa Rice Ltd. Some people did not like that. But there were 1000 rice farmers in Vanua Levu. They have no other livelihood and if we hadn't revived the Rewa Rice company those 1000 families would have become destitute.

Some people who are importing rice into this country and who are making a lot of money out of that did not like that because they said they will not be able to make a lot of money if Rewa Rice company comes back into operation. They don't want to care about what those 1000 families will do, how their children and wives will live, what they will eat. But this government cares about them. We care for the people, that is why we did that. It cost the people $4.5 million to start Rewa Rice again. But this is the government that puts people before money. That is why we did that.

Another reason for agriculture development is that land in this country is largely owned by our Fijian brothers and sisters. Now much of that land is lying idle and undeveloped, except in the sugarcane belt. A lot of other land is not put to productive use. The government's strategies are to see that by investing money in agriculture we will encourage our Fijian brothers and sisters to develop their land so that they can earn income from that development. They can become commercial farmers, land which they did not need, once they develop it they can lease it and earn an income from lease money.

And for that we have created additional resources and all those land owners who are willing to have their land developed can use this money to develop that. And this is one way of addressing Fijian poverty in the rural areas because they have a resource there which they can develop and earn incomes out of. This is another reason for pouring money into agriculture.

I can go on for the rest of the night telling you what government has done to help the poor, help revive economic development. Mr Krishna Dutt has told you that he has confirmed most of our promises inside the last 12 months. But much work needs to be done.

Our latest priority at this time is to unite our nation. That is very important. Because a nation that is divided, which is split, will not progress. No matter where you are. We have seen this even in the developed world where the inter-ethnic conflict and other unfortunate events have crippled much greater nations, much more advanced and richer that Fiji.

Fiji's only hope (and hope) for all her people is that we all come together as brothers and sisters, as citizens with common interest, with a common goal. Everybody's rights and interests, traditions, customs and cultures are protected under the Constitution. Let nobody fool you that your custom is under threat, your religion is under threat, that your land may be taken away from you, that you might lose your property. No.

Let me remind those people who are protesting today, that they were the very ones who put through the 1997 Constitution when they were in power. And under that very Constitution the rights and interests of all communities are firmly secure. Moreover, the rights and interests of our indigenous community — the Fijian and Rotumans take precedence over the rights and interests of other communities should there be a conflict of interest between the rights and interests of the Fijian community and those of other communities.

Now that having been done, we saw what happened to this country after the 1987 coups. We all suffered in the process, everybody, not a single one did not suffer. Maybe some didn't, those who created this mischief. But by and large, all of us suffered — Indians, Fijians, Chinese. We all suffered to some degree and the consequence of that: the country suffered because the economy plunged. Jobs were lost, our currency devalued, everything became very dear. Government did not have enough money to provide for good health services, education, to build and repair roads, to help the poor.

And it took us 12 long years to build back. We put through a new Constitution in 1997. It came into force in 1998. It is a Constitution which seeks to unite the people of the country, irrespective of race. It is a Constitution that provides for power sharing. Our government is made up of four political parties. It is not a Labour government. It is a People's Coalition government. We have the Labour Party, the Fijian Association Party, the Christian Democrat Alliance, and the Party of National Unity. And of course, we have the General Voters Party who joined us after the elections. We have one or two independents as well. Out of 71 members in Parliament, 58 sit on our side.

So it is a very representative government. No one can accuse it of being a government of one race. And we took special pains to reassure our Fijian brothers and sisters. As Prime Minister, I appointed 12 Fijians to my Cabinet and only six Indians. Because for the first time, the nation was to have a non-Fijian Prime Minister.

In such a situation, it was very important that I retain the trust and confidence of the Fijian people. I also invited that time the SVT party to join the government because they had a constitutional right. Under the Constitution, any party which wins 10 per cent or more of the seats is entitled to be represented in Cabinet. I did invite them to join the government. But they stipulated conditions which were very difficult for any reasonable government to accept. And by choice they decided to stay out of the government. Otherwise they would have been part of the government also.

Now we also have a major party, the National Federation Party. That party is not represented in Parliament any more. They had a coalition with the SVT party. And when they went into the election, they went on a platform also of multi-racialism. But after they lost the elections, SVT has changed. It is no longer espousing multi-racial principles. In fact, they have become very racial. One can see that in Parliament too, in debate and directions and all that. On account of that I am wondering whether the NFP remains part of that coalition. Because we have to be honest with ourselves.

We cannot play politics with the lives of innocent people. And we don't do that. We went to these elections, and ever since the formation of the Labour

Party, we had a dream, a vision about Fiji. We want to see a prosperous and united country. It has great people and great potential. It will all come together. Nobody will want to go to Australia and New Zealand. We can create those conditions right here in Fiji But only if we can come together.

So that is the vision with which we have been working ever since 1985 when I entered politics for the first time. And that is the vision that has driven us and my colleagues. We have a vision for Fiji. We want to see a united and prosperous Fiji where there is love, there is sharing and caring for each other, and where the nation has enough resources to provide for every one.

After all what does the human being want. What do you want? Whether you be a Fijian, an Indian or Chinese, what do you want? What do you really want from life? What you want is to be happy. Everybody wants to be happy, and to be happy you must be able to satisfy your daily needs. If you have children you must be able to provide for them. You must have a place called home, a roof over your heads, you must have clothes to wear. You must have three meals a day. You must have a job which brings you the income from which you can provide for your children. You want the government to provide for education for your children and good health services and water and electricity.

If you have all of these you are a contented person. That is what one expects from life. If you are able to meet your daily needs, your family is happy, your children get a good education, they are able to get a good job. That is what everybody wants. And that is the responsibility of government. Then we provide these things for our people. (Clapping)

But we cannot do that unless we come together. Government can only do so much. What government can do depends on its ability, on the financial resources that it has at its disposal, but the economy does not just run on that. The economy runs on how productively we use the resources at our disposal. And if our economy is doing well then people will be doing well, too, so long as you help the government there which believes in fair distribution of wealth. This is the vision we have of Fiji. And we can do it if we can come together. There are issues that they are addressing in those marches. They are not the real issues affecting the Fijians. No. Their real issues are what I am saying.

We were ready to debate in Parliament, we are currently debating the Social Justice Bill, affirmative action. What the government can do to help the disadvantaged people in education, housing, land and all that the Constitution requires the Parliament to do. An act of legislation for affirmative action for the disadvantaged people in our community and actually the contribution from a number of members of the opposition was quite sickening.

They are pointing at the problems faced by Fijian people — Fijian poverty, eductation, in commerce etc. These are the problems of the Fijian people. I know that. We have known that for a long time and we have got programs and ideas on how to address those problems. But they make it sound as if these problems were created when we came to power. That is only 12 months ago.

And I said they are thinking as if for the last 30 years since independence, for 29 years we have had a Fijian Prime Minister. If I have to take the blame, I will take one-thirtieth of the blame. Not more than that. The rest of the blame must be taken by those people.

But you see the way they whip up the emotions. It is not fair. So this is what they are trying to do at the moment. Quite wrongly, they are distorting things. They are telling outright lies even in Parliament. And with this kind of leadership, this kind of behaviour, we will never be able to build a nation. It is a very basic thing that one cannot attain happiness by making others unhappy. You can't do that. We will never be happy if you want to make others unhappy. You yourself will not get justice if you are not just to others. And this is the message that is there in every scripture, every prophet's message, in every religion. We are all God's children. Whether we are born Fijian, Indian, Chinese or a European. We don't decide. He decides. So why can't we, as all His children, live in peace and harmony?

In every democratic nation, people have the right to choose their government. You have chosen a government. Many people pray that the government will do good. God has given you a government, support that government. Because they are there to do good for you, for all of us.

But if every time we lose an election, we want to change the Constitution of the country, we will not get anywhere. The world is moving ahead very fast, we have entered the 21st century. This is a world of technology. We have got to move forward with that world. If we have to take our Fijian brothers and sisters with us, we have to work overtime for them. Because they must become a part of this fast-moving world. And we cannot do that by keeping the nation divided by wanting to feed on non-existent racial prejudice, things that don't exist, which are just invented by people for their own best reasons.

I will talk to you about these things because they too concern me, that they must be concerning you. I know for the last few weeks you have seen all this. You must be thinking about this. Many of you may be thinking what is our future, how secure are we. Don't despair because inherently there is a lot of goodness in our people. We all owe our allegiance to Fiji. We are Fiji's children and whatever we must do for the good of this land, for the good of this country, that is like a mother to us. So in all our action, thoughts and needs, we must think like that.

We have been trying very hard in the government to move the economy because, at the end of the day, it is a growing, vibrant and healthy economy that will deliver.

We don't have an economy that is growing, that is vibrant. We cannot help the poor, we cannot give the jobs that our young men and women are dying for, we cannot give you good roads, we cannot give you a good water supply, we can't give you good education, we can't give you good health services. Everything depends on how an economy does. That is where the prosperity comes from.

And that will only come, as I said, if we work together and utilise both our human resource and others. And this is what this government is trying to do, trying to move the country forward, address the problems that we have faced, help the poor, develop agriculture, tourism and other sectors of the economy so that we can provide a better life for ourselves. That is the aim of your government and that is what we will carry on doing. So I ask you tonight to have faith, confidence and trust in your own selves, and in this country.

COUP

Life has never been easy but we can make it easy if we all do the right thing. So that is my appeal to you tonight and from time to time we will be coming and visiting you and we will be keeping you informed of what the government does.

CONFIDENTIAL DRAFT AND STATEMENT OF 22 MAY 2000

George Speight

Excellency:

I am writing on behalf of the group of indigenous Fijians who took over the Parliament of Fiji on Friday 19 May 2000. The illegal and unconstitutional action that was taken is acknowledged. It represented a year's efforts on the part of a wide spectrum of the indigenous community to bring to the attention of the Government, our increasing concern in the way the People's Coalition government began to address issues that are of fundamental importance to the indigenous community of Fiji.

For example, the nature of the tenancy of indigenous-owned land to Indo-Fijian cane farmers, the progressive removal of affirmative action for the indigenous community which has lagged behind in every sector of the Fiji economy — in education, in commerce, in the professions, in management, in technical staff, etc.

The 1997 Constitution was rejected by eight of the fourteen Fijian provinces, however by a combination of parliamentary and not-so-parliamentary manoeuvring, the Great Council of Chiefs approved the amended Constitution. In fact, the 1997 Constitution is not an amendment of the 1990 Constitution but represents a brand new Constitution.

To compound this serious error in judgement on the part of the indigenous political leadership, the SVT government with lack of foresight and prudence, at the tail end of its administration, introduced a completely new electoral legislation. Worse still, it did not give itself sufficient time, nor made any effort to understand the complications to the new electoral law.

There was also at this point of time, a growing discontent on the part of segments of the indigenous community. There was a 'ganging up' of at least two indigenous parties in its allocation of their preferences which ultimately led to the defeat not only of the SVT-led political party but also of the National Federation Party (NFP) which had been the premier party, overseeing the interests of the Indo-Fijian community over the last 30 years.

The People's Coalition Party was the major beneficiary of the Constitution and the new electoral legislation. Of the 71 seats in Parliament the Fiji Labour Party won 35 seats. With the support of other parties it was able to control some 61 seats in Parliament. The government that was subsequently formed comprises the Fiji Labour Party, the Fijian Association and two other smaller parties.

One of the basic concerns of the indigenous people when the draft of the Constitution was being discussed was the likely loss of indigenous political leadership and control. The indigenous people remain distrustful of the Indo-Fijian political intentions. The subsequent events following the formation of the People's Coalition government in May 1999 confirmed and convinced indigenous body politic that their fears and trepidation of Indo-Fijian political leadership were well founded.

The SVT party, which lost the election, won only eight seats even though they obtained 38 per cent of the votes. One small indigenous party which won 9 per cent of the votes was given two seats in Cabinet. Another indigenous party which won 19 per cent of the vote was given a Deputy Prime Minister post plus three other Cabinet positions. A provincial-based indigenous party was given two Cabinet seats. The SVT party, which had won 38 per cent of the votes, had given certain conditions when it was invited to join the government. Understandably the Prime Minister, the Hon. Mahendra P. Chaudhry rejected the response of the SVT.

If the Prime Minister were to lead the country successfully he would have allowed the dust to settle, temperatures to cool, and then come back for a dialogue with the party that represented 38 per cent of the electorate.

Over the last 12 months the indigenous people have watched, with dismay, concern and resentment, Mr Chaudhry's blatant attempt to weaken, or if possible destroy important indigenous institutions, namely the Native Land Trust Board (NLTB) and the Great Council of Chiefs (GCC).

Of course central to indigenous concern is their land. The indigenous people of Fiji own some 86 per cent of the land. But the ownership is not by individuals but by clans (Mataqali). In fact every indigenous generation has the right of usage of the land for which they have. It is their obligation to ensure the land, which the clan owns, is protected and passed on to the next generation.

It is interesting to note though that some of the best land has been completely alienated to private ownership, or has been used by Indo-Fijian cane farmers for the last 100–120 years. The lease fees for these lands, under cane farming, to put it charitably, are miserable. In the last 25 years, for instance, Fiji has been allowed to sell 160,000 tonnes of sugar to the European Union, at a rate that is three to four times the world price. Not a cent of this windfall has been given to the indigenous landowners, apart from their uneconomic lease fee. Moreover, it should be noted that over the years cane farmers owe a substantial amount of arrears to the NLTB.

The Agriculture and Landlord Tenancy Act (ALTA) which originally came as the Agriculture and Landlord Tenants Ordinance (ALTO) is now coming to an end. Under the Act, farmers were given 30 years to lease the land. Every farmer that entered a leasing arrangement, under the Act, knew that he had 30 years to farm the land, after which the lease expires. When the lease expires, unless the landowners wish to renew the lease, the tenants have to move out. Since 1997 or thereabouts, a number of farms under the ALTA arrangement have had their leases expire, and tenants are expected to go elsewhere if the indigenous landowners decide not to renew the lease.

COUP

Since Mr Chaudhry came to power he has attempted to coerce the NLTB to continue granting leases to tenants under ALTA. This goes right against the face of a clearly stated policy of the Great Council of Chiefs and the NLTB that any renewal of leases will come under the Native Land Trust Act. As far as indigenous landowners are concerned, ALTA must and should be repealed. As far as the indigenous landowners are concerned ALTA is dead. Yet Mr Chaudhry has continued to fight the indigenous landowners on this issue. He seems unable to accept that the indigenous landowners have the right to decide the terms and conditions on which their land can be leased.

The Fiji Labour Party, since 1987, has advocated the establishment of a Land Use Commission. The late Dr Timoci Bavadra, who subsequently became Prime Minister when the Fiji Labour Party won the election in 1987, first presented the proposal to the Great Council of Chiefs. Since the government came to power in 1999 one of the most important elements in its policy platform is the establishment of a Land Use Commission.

Again the NLTB representing the indigenous landowners rejected this proposal. What is worse is that the Government, i.e. PM Chaudhry with his usual arrogance, which has become the trademark of his style of political leadership, is dismissive of the stand taken by the NLTB and his insistence that Land Use Commission be established in spite of the indigenous landowners opposition.

In fact, in an attempt to hoodwink and subvert traditional indigenous leadership, a representative group of indigenous chiefs was sent by PM Chaudhry to observe traditional land ownership in Sarawak, Malaysia.

The troubling aspect of the Chaudhry-led Government is its ongoing attempt to divide the indigenous people of Fiji. He has certainly mastered the tactics of divide and rule. For some time the previous government (SVT) had to put in place policy initiatives to assist the indigenous community to 'catch up', particularly in the field of education, and commerce, where indigenous participation is non-existent. Indeed, when one reflects on the debate that led to the passage of the 1997 Constitution, the Indo-Fijian political parties conceded absolutely nothing particularly in the field of commercial participation where their community holds all the cards.

coup

Even before the People's Coalition Party came to power, Mr Chaudhry was leading opposition spokesperson, who was always critical of affirmative action in favour of the indigenous community. And Mr Chaudhry, when he came to power saw that this affirmative action, in favour of the indigenous community, was removed. In its place, the social justice provisions of the 1997 Constitution were implemented with unbelievable speed and lack of consideration and consultation with the indigenous community. And now every community in Fiji will be put on an equal basis in spite of the fact that the Indo-Fijian community controls the economy.

The events that took place on 19 May, 2000 represent the culmination of 12 months of frustration, anger, disappointment and outrage in the manner in which the Chaudhry government dealt with matters of importance to the indigenous community. What is worse is that the nine indigenous Ministers in the Cabinet, two of whom are Deputy PM appear to be completely 'under the thumb' of the PM. They are, to put it elegantly, impotent almost to the point of being eunuchs in their ability and failure to safeguard what was perceived by the indigenous community as important to them. In fairness to the indigenous Cabinet Ministers the above judgement may appear to be unduly harsh. It would seem that none of the indigenous Ministers was ever able to articulate, either privately or publicly, what was important to the indigenous electorate, which they purport to represent and which elected them to Parliament.

It is useful to view the current crisis in Fiji in the context of numbers. The indigenous people of Fiji represent some 51 per cent of the Fiji population of approximately 790,000. From a global perspective, the indigenous population of Fiji does not merely have to deal with the 300,000 Indo-Fijians who are now citizens of the country. Against this number the indigenous community of Fiji have to take cognisance of the one billion people of India itself, and a substantial number of people of Indian origin in other parts of the world, notable Mauritius, Trinidad, Guyana and parts of East Africa. As well as this group, there are those who man some of the most important international institutions, such as the World Bank, the IMF and the United Nations system for development.

coup

As an indigeous people, we are part of the world's indigenous communities whose interests and precarious (some of whch borders on extinction) were singled out for special attention by the international community through declaration, the Decade of Indigenous People. Indeed, the indigenous people of Fiji are under threat and this dangerous threat is being undertaken by a government that was constitutionally elected and uses the provisions of the Constitution that would put in place laws that would bring greater disadvantage to the indigenous comunity of Fiji.

This letter is an attempt to provide your Excellency with a background of why the events of 19 May, 2000 had taken place. There is no going back. If the indigenous community do not assert their rights now and with regency, to govern their own country, they will in next to no time become history. The indigenous people of Fiji are not alone in this precarious position. Even the indigenous communities in our largest South Pacific states often find the going difficult.

The President of Fiji's dismissal of the genuine concerns of the indigenous community compounds the impasse of the last two days. The President appears reluctant to address these real and growing concerns.

The events of 19 May, 2000 could have been avoided if Mr Chaudhry had the ability and political courage to listen to the growing unrest of the indigenous people and step down. The country would have avoided all trouble if in his place a leader was appointed who would at least listen and dialogue with the indigenous people with urgency, from the start of his administration. In fact, from all his recent public statements, PM Chaudhry dismissed the marches as being the work of agitators and those who could not accept that they had lost the election. The present crisis lies squarely at the door of Mr Chaudhry, whose arrogance and refusal to listen to other viewpoints, contrary to his, are hallmarks of his style of governance. This of course is nothing new to those who knew him in his days in the Opposition. Chaudhry banked very much on the fact that he had an absolute majority in Parliament, and that sufficient mandate to run 'rough shod' over the concerns of the indigenous community.

Added to this, the grievance of the indigenous community was that the President ignored the grounds of dissatisfaction of the indigenous community as expressed throughout the media over the last 12 months. This then led to two public demonstrations which were then subsequently followed by a third demonstration that culminated in the entry of representatives of the indigenous people into Parliament.

There is no denying that the events of 19 May 2000 represent an assault of democracy and constitutionality. The events represented 'the last straw' to many members of the indigenous community. It was not meant to be vengeance nor violent. Those who did what they did on 19 May 2000 did so because it was the only way available to them to bring to the attention of the powers that be that the concerns of the indigenous community are real and need to be addressed with urgency.

It is well within the moral high position of the President of Fiji to persuade the PM and his government to voluntarily resign. It would give the opportunity, under the State of Emergency, to appoint an Interim Government drawn from all major political parties. The task of such a government is first and foremost to address the grievances of the indigenous community in the light of the 1997 Constitution. Unfortunately, to date, the President appears reluctant to adopt this path that could lead to immediate stability, reconciliation among the major communities, economic growth and development. This would be well within the legal powers of the President of Fiji since he has declared a State of Emergency. Such prudent and statesman-like action would have found acceptance and approval by the international community.

STATEMENT TO THE COMMONWEALTH BY THE FIJI PEOPLE'S COALITION GOVERNMENT

Hon. Pratap Chand and Hon. Jokapeci Koroi

A statement made to the Secretary-General, Commonwealth Secretariat, Mr Don McKinnon, and Members of the Commonwealth Ministerial Action Group

Introduction

We submit the following statement for urgent consideration by the Commonwealth Ministerial Action Group, scheduled to meet on 6 June 2000.

We regard the convening of the CMAG meeting as a clear and very welcome signal of the level of concern shown by the Commonwealth about the current crisis in the Fiji Islands, in particular the unlawful and unconstitutional overthrow of the democratically elected People's Coalition government by terrorists on Friday 19 May, and the holding of our Prime Minister and Government as hostages for the past two weeks.

Brief overview of developments since 19 May 2000

(i) the principal demands of the terrorists led by Speight were the dismissal of the Prime Minister and the elected Government; the abrogation of the Constitution; amnesty for Speight and co-conspirators; the establishment of ethnic Fijian paramountcy within a new constitution; and the appointment of a new exclusively ethnic Fijian Government. Speight has persistently insisted the release of the hostages was conditional on these demands being met.

(ii) Following the takeover of Parliament and the taking of hostages including the Prime Minister and members of his Cabinet, the Coalition pledged its support to the President in his decision to assume executive authority and to declare a state of emergency. This course of action appeared to be the best possible alternative in view of the crisis facing the country at the time.

(iii) On Saturday 27 May, following resolutions of the Bose Levu Vakaturaga (Council of Chiefs), the President adopted a course of action which resulted in the dismissal of the Prime Minister and Cabinet and the suspension of Parliament. The Government rejected this course of action and made its position clear to the President. We argued that it would have the effect of legitimising the overthrow of a constitutional and democratically elected government by terrorists.

In support of our position, we submitted to the President copies of three opinions by international constitutional experts, all of which confirmed that the President's powers under the Constitution did not extend to the dismissal of the Prime Minister and his Cabinet or the suspension of the Parliament. His actions were unequivocally unlawful and unconstitutional.

(iv) The dismissal of the Prime Minister by the President followed resolutions passed by the Bose Levu Vakaturaga (Council of Chiefs). The constitutional powers of the BLV are in fact restricted to the appointment of 14 members of the Senate (section 64 (1) a), and the appointment and removal of the President (s.90 and s.93). We advised the President of these limitations on the BLV's powers.

In essence, the BLV does NOT have the power to remove the government or the Prime Minister. Nor does it have the authority to demand or endorse any political configuration that follows from such action.

(v) Following the takeover of Parliament, supporters of the terrorists plunged the country into orchestrated violence, looting, arson, ransacking, hijacking of vehicles, and other shocking acts of terrorism, targeting innocent people and whole communities — especially Indo-Fijians.

(vi) The military intervention this week was ostensibly aimed at restoring law and order. The Coalition totally rejects this argument. Firstly, the military did not intervene to restore law and order when the Government was unlawfully taken captive by the terrorists. Moreover, during the 10 days that ensued after the takeover, the military demonstrated very clearly that it was unwilling to restore law and order.

Secondly, the military has taken the drastic and quite unnecessary action of removing the President, assuming executive authority itself, and abrogating the Constitution. Further, it has offered an amnesty to the terrorists and engaged in negotiations with them about the composition of an interim military-appointed government as well as the process of developing a new Constitution. The military has agreed to a number of Speight's choices for the proposed interim government.

We reject all these actions taken by the Fiji Military Forces as unlawful and unconstitutional. They make it abundantly clear that the military has a clear political agenda that goes well beyond its professed intention to restore law and order.

(vii) The actions taken by the President, the BLV and the Fiji Military Forces have not been directed at solving the hostage crisis, upholding the Constitution, and restoring the democratically elected government. On the contrary, they manifestly support the principal demands of the terrorists which were aimed at unlawfully overthrowing a democratic government and the Constitution, in furtherance of the personal agendas of a few agitators.

People's Coalition Submission

(i) We wish to remind the CMAG of the special features of the Fiji Islands Constitution and its respected standing in the international community, especially in the Commonwealth, for its commitment to the core international principles of equality, non-discrimination, human rights, and social and economic rights.

At the heart of our Constitution lies a very comprehensive Bill of Rights, including unparalleled provisions on racial discrimination and torture. We are very proud of this.

In terms of process, the Constitution is the product of five years of consultations and consensus building. The specific content is the product of joint negotiations between all political parties, and they took place under the former SVT government and its Prime Minister, Rabuka (who has this week been appointed by the FMF Commander as a member of the Military Council of Advisers). The Constitution was unanimously approved by both houses of Fiji's Parliament, and the Council of Chiefs, and subsequently endorsed by the Commonwealth.

The origins of our Constitution are grounded in the painful lessons of the 1987 coups. The overriding purpose was to ensure that we never had to endure the horrors of a coup again. Another key objective was to give an unequivocal constitutional commitment to addressing issues of concern that emerged in 1987 including ethnic disparities and the need to include strong provisions for affirmative action on behalf of indigenous Fijians, and the further constitutional entrenchment of the protection of indigenous rights.

Indeed the constitution is hailed as an exemplary model for the protection and advancement of indigenous rights by the international community.

(ii) We are now effectively dealing with an illegal and unconstitutional overthrow of government, supported by various institutions of the state, including the military, and the unlawful abrogation of our Constitution. Any international support for the recent (or future) actions of the Fiji Military Forces outside its 'law and order' mandate would legitimise the overthrow of democracy and constitutional government. It would give recognition to an unlawful and unconstitutional regime.

(iii) The overthrow of a constitutional and democratically elected government by the military (through the support of a terrorist group using hostages) offends international standards including the core civil and political rights embraced by the Commonwealth. As you well know,

COUP

these cherished principles have been restated and enhanced over the last decade, especially through the Millbrook Commonwealth Action Programme.

(iv) It is crucial that the integrity of these international commitments to democracy, good governance, human rights and the rule of law are vigilantly defended by the Commonwealth. The Harare Commonwealth Declaration now stands fundamentally violated in the Fiji Islands. The situation demands an urgent and principled response by the Commonwealth, through the CMAG.

Failure to do this will without doubt result in:

- a total breakdown of law and order and a descent into anarchy
- a rapid degeneration into institutionalised racial discrimination
- ethnic persecution and serious human rights violations both by the security forces and armed vigilante groups
- victimisation and harassment of government members and supporters, and the Indo-Fijian community in general
- a flaring-up of hostile provincialism (tribalism) within the ethnic Fijian community including the setting up of a separate state by the western provinces which strongly supports the elected People's Coalition government
- a rapid decline in the integrity of Fiji's judiciary, public service and all accountability institutions.

(v) We have high, and we know justified, hopes that the CMAG and the Commonwealth will give a clear and decisive commitment to being the principal intermediary in securing a satisfactory outcome of the crisis, consistent with our Constitution and the Harare Principles.

Specifically, we ask you to invoke your mandate and related operational machinery to help restore the constitutional and democratically elected government and uphold our Constitution.

(vi) We therefore look to the CMAG to take action along the following lines:

- Continue to recognise the People's Coalition under the leadership of Prime Minister Mahendra Chaudhry as the legitimate Government of the Fiji Islands. This would be consistent with the Commonwealth's decision on Sierra Leone in 1997. It would also be in line with the principles of the Harare Declaration.

- Warn the Fiji Military Forces that its failure to restore the democratically elected People's Coalition government and the 1997 Constitution will result in the imposition of the full force of the Commonwealth and international sanctions against the illegal regime set up by the Fiji Military Forces.

- Specify that these sanctions will include

  i) Fiji's expulsion from the Commonwealth

  ii) A unified suspension of diplomatic relations with the illegal regime set up by the Fiji Military Forces by member states

  iii) Suspension of technical assistance, development aid and other assistance or support by member states and the Commonwealth Secretariat

  iv) A Commonwealth commitment to pursuing further diplomatic, political and economic isolation of the illegal regime through the United Nations and other international agencies.

If this does not happen by the time of your meeting on Monday (6 June 2000), we ask that the CMAG call for the unconditional and immediate release of hostages.

If the Fiji Military Forces do not restore the elected government and the 1997 Constitution, we ask that the Commonwealth take necessary measures in response, including the setting up and rapid deployment of a peacekeeping force.

We stress the need to act now, without further delay, before the situation deteriorates very rapidly.

Conclusion

Our Government and the vast majority of Fiji citizens of all ethnic groups cherish our membership of the Commonwealth. In our time of crisis, we look to the Commonwealth to uphold the integrity of its Charter and, accordingly, to take firm, decisive and principled action to help restore constitutional government in our beloved country.

STATEMENT TO MEMBERS OF THE COMMONWEALTH MINISTERIAL GROUP

Felix Anthony

Introduction

The Fiji Trades Union Congress, through the Commonwealth Trade Union Council, submits the following statement for urgent consideration by the Commonwealth Ministerial Action Group meeting on Fiji.

We welcome the CMAG meeting. It demonstrates the level of concern shown by the Commonwealth at the unlawful and unconstitutional overthrow of the democratically elected People's Coalition government.

The People's Coalition government is a coalition of the Fiji Labour Party, the Fijian Association Party, the VLV and the Party of National Unity. In the first election held following the overwhelming acceptance of Fiji's new constitution, the People's Coalition won 55 seats in Fiji's Parliament. Within the Coalition, the Fiji Labour Party was the largest grouping with 37 members.

The FTUC has close links with the Fiji Labour Party and several of our former leaders are now a part of the Cabinet. Clearly, the People's Coalition has a massive mandate given to it in May 1999. Such a decisive mandate had not been given to any elected government since Fiji's independence in 1970. We, the workers of this country of all ethnic groups, are proud partners in Fiji's governance through the Fiji Labour Party. The People's Coalition was speedily delivering on its program of government. It is this success that most explains the actions of terrorists and others supporting them.

Background

(i) The key demands of the terrorists led by Speight were

- the dismissal of the Prime Minister and the elected government;
- dismissal of the President;
- the abrogation of the Constitution;
- amnesty for Speight and other terrorists;
- the establishment of ethnic Fijian domination through a new constitution;
- and the appointment of a new exclusively ethnic Fijian Government until a new constitution is approved.

Speight has persistently insisted the release of the hostages was conditional on these demands being met — restating them only this evening (5 June).

The narrative below shows most of these demands have already been met. It shows the military's complicity with Speight's cause.

(ii) Following the takeover of Parliament and the taking of hostages including the Prime Minister and members of his Cabinet, the FTUC pledged its support to the President in his decision to assume executive authority and to declare a state of emergency. This course of action appeared logical given that the state of emergency was constitutionally declared.

(iii) However, on Saturday 27 May, following resolutions of the Bose Levu Vakaturaga (Council of Chiefs), the President went beyond this and dismissed the Prime Minister and Cabinet and suspended the Parliament. This effectively was giving in to the first of the demands of Speight and his supporters — i.e. the removal of the People's Coalition government.

(iv) The dismissal of the Prime Minister by the President followed resolutions passed by the Bose Levu Vakaturaga (Council of Chiefs). The

BLV has no constitutional functions with respect to dismissal or appointment of government. It has an advisory role to play in constitutional matters. With respect to the Constitution itself, the BLV had given its unanimous endorsement to the Constitution in early 1997.

(v) Following the takeover of Parliament, supporters of the terrorists plunged the country into orchestrated human rights abuses targeting innocent people and whole communities — especially Indo-Fijians. Workers and farmers have borne the brunt of this violence and human rights abuses. Reports on human rights abuses have been now relayed to the Secretary General separately. The links between terrorists, security forces and vigilante groups have been well documented.

(vi) The military intervention was aimed at restoring law and order. But following the declaration of martial law, the military abrogated the 1997 Constitution. By abrogating the Constitution, the military gave in to two other principal demands of Speight and co-conspirators, i.e., the removal of the President and the abrogation of the Constitution.

The military's action in assuming executive authority itself and abrogating the Constitution is totally unnecessary. Further, it has offered an amnesty to the terrorists and engaged in negotiations with them about the framework for a new constitution — two of the other demands of the terrorists.

It is clear that the military has a political agenda that goes well beyond its objective of restoring law and order. It has obvious sympathies with Speight and his group. It has committed itself to preparing a constitution that will enshrine indigenous Fijian domination. It has agreed to a course of action that will allow Speight and his men to be a part of government in the near future.

The military's abrogation of the Constitution has no support in Fiji society. It is condemned by the Fiji Trades Union Congress, the People's Coalition government, by the Fiji Law Society, by the Vice President of Fiji and many chiefs throughout the country, by a whole range of civil society organisations. It has no legitimacy therefore.

COUP

(vii)The sequence of actions taken by the President, the BLV and the Fiji Military Forces have not been directed at solving the hostage crisis, upholding the Constitution, and restoring the democratically elected government. On the contrary, they further the principal demands of the terrorists, which were aimed at unlawfully overthrowing a democratic government and the Constitution.

Fiji Trades Union Congress Position

i)   We remind the CMAG and the international community that workers and Fiji's civil society cherish their Constitution. The Constitution is deeply committed to the principles of equality, non-discrimination, human rights, and social and economic rights. It protects and enhances core labour rights. At the heart is the comprehensive Bill of Rights, including its unparalleled provisions on racial discrimination and equality.

ii) The Constitution is the product of five years of consensus building. The specific content is the product of negotiations between all political parties. Both houses of Fiji's Parliament and the Council of Chiefs unanimously approved the Constitution. But even more importantly, a large segment of Fiji society, its non-governmental organisations, trade unions and civic groups directly participated in the constitution-building process. They all have a special sense of ownership over this Constitution.

iii) A key objective of the Constitution was its commitment to protecting and enhancing the rights and interests of the indigenous community. Firm constitutional provisions were made for affirmative action to reduce ethnic disparities.

iv) The Council of Chiefs was given constitutional recognition and granted the sole constitutional authority to appoint the President. The Council of Chiefs' nominees in the Senate were given an absolute constitutional veto on matters affecting indigenous Fijian rights and interests, including land matters. Fiji's Constitution is hailed internationally as an exemplary model for the protection and advancement of indigenous rights.

The abrogation of the Constitution means that there is now an illegal and unconstitutional overthrow of democratic and constitutional government. Any international support for the recent (or future) actions of the Fiji Military Forces would legitimise the overthrow of democracy and constitutional government. It would give recognition to an unlawful and unconstitutional regime.

The overthrow of a constitutional and democratically elected government by the military (through the support of a terrorist group using hostages) offends core civil and political rights reflected in the Harare Declaration.

It is crucial that the integrity of the Commonwealth's commitment to democracy, good governance, human rights and the rule of law are vigilantly defended. The Harare Commonwealth Declaration now stands fundamentally violated in the Fiji Islands. The situation demands an urgent response by the CMAG.

v) Fiji now stares at a total breakdown of law and order, a degeneration into institutionalised racial discrimination, ethnic persecution and serious human rights violations by both the security forces and armed vigilante groups, victimisation and harassment of government members and trade unions, and the Indo-Fijian community in general. Fiji faces the prospect of hostile provincialism. The western provinces which strongly support the elected People's Coalition government are now proceeding with the setting up of an independent state and government.

vi) We are also witnessing a rapid decline in the integrity of Fiji's judiciary, public service and accountability institutions. Fiji's independent Public Service Commission has now been terminated; several judges have already resigned. The public service is being rapidly radicalised as is reflected through the most recent appointments to Fiji's missions abroad.

vii) Workers in Fiji ask that the CMAG give a clear and decisive commitment to helping secure a satisfactory outcome of the crisis, consistent with Fiji's Constitution and the Harare Principles.

viii)Specifically, we ask that the CMAG take firm and decisive steps to help restore the constitutional and democratically elected government and uphold our Constitution.

We therefore look to the CMAG to take action along the following lines:

ix) Continue to recognise the People's Coalition under the leadership of Prime Minister Mahendra Chaudhry as the legitimate government of the Fiji Islands. This would be consistent with the principles of the Harare Declaration.

Warn the Fiji Military Forces that their failure to restore the democratically elected People's Coalition government and the 1997 Constitution in a reasonable time frame will result in the imposition of the full force of the Commonwealth and international sanctions against the illegal regime set up by the Fiji Military Forces.

Impose an immediate ban on travel to any Commonwealth country:

· of Speight and all members of his interim government,
· all members of the military's Council of Advisers
· heads of public service.

Specify that should the democratically elected government not be restored within two months, the sanctions will include:

i) Fiji's expulsion from the Commonwealth;
ii) A unified suspension of diplomatic relations with the illegal regime set up by the Fiji Military Forces by member states;
iii) Suspension of technical assistance, development aid and other assistance or support by member states and the Commonwealth Secretariat;
iv) Activating a comprehensive trade, sporting, travel, cultural and educational regime of sanctions;
v) Total freeze on all links with Fiji Government, its public service, the military and other institutions;

vi) A Commonwealth commitment to pursuing further diplomatic, political and economic isolation of the illegal regime through the United Nations and other international agencies;

vii) A commitment to pursuing leaders of any unconstitutional government and Speight and his supporters for human rights abuses under international law, a freezing of their assets in Commonwealth countries.

We further ask that the CMAG call for the unconditional and immediate release of hostages.

If the Fiji Military Forces do not restore the elected government and the 1997 Constitution within two months, we ask that the Commonwealth take necessary measures in response, including the setting up and rapid deployment of a stabilising/peacekeeping force.

We stress the need to act now before the situation deteriorates very rapidly.

Conclusion

Workers, their trade unions and the vast majority or ordinary citizens of Fiji cherish Fiji's membership of the Commonwealth. They look to the Commonwealth to take firm and principled action to help restore constitutional government in our beloved country.

We plead that the Commonwealth's actions be decisive so that the armed overthrow of democratically elected governments can be brought to an end. Let there be no mistake about it. The coup underway in the Solomon Islands today (5 June 2000) directly flows from the coup in Fiji.

Terrorists and armed men seem to have the view that the resolve of the Commonwealth and the international community will be weak and eventually they will come to terms with a new political order established through the force of guns.

STATEMENT OF THE METHODIST CHURCH IN FIJI AND ROTUMA ON THE ARMED SEIZURE OF GOVERNMENT

Iliatia Sevati Tuwere

The Methodist Church in Fiji and Rotuma appeals to George Speight, his group and supporters to free the hostages they hold in the Parliament complex in Suva. The Church recognises and accepts the reality of the situation and speaks on the issue from this perspective. It condemns the illegal takeover of Mr Mahendra Chaudhry's government as well as the inhumane and degrading treatment of its members by being held in captivity. It denounces the destruction and looting of businesses in Suva and other areas, the loss of the life of a policeman in rioting in the city, and lawlessness in other parts of the nation. The Church extends its sympathy to members of the Indian community for being targeted in the mass attacks, destruction and looting.

The Church supports His Excellency the President, Ratu Sir Kamisese Mara, and the Great Council of Chiefs in their efforts to break the stalemate in the hostage situation and to craft a constitutional and just solution to the political crisis. We believe the President's decision to step aside for 21 days to allow martial law to be imposed in the nation is necessary, because of the rapid deterioration in the law and order situation. On our assessment, this step must be taken to impose the rule of law and to restore constitutional government.

We are saddened and ashamed of the lawlessness and violence. We take the responsibility of failing to teach our people, who make up the majority of the perpetrators and supporters in these unlawful activities. But the Church believes something bigger is happening in this crisis — it is about cultural understanding. More effort and energy should be directed at cultivating cultural understanding. We hope that in the near future the Indian community can find forgiveness for their attackers and look beyond the anger and frustration of this moment, to explore, articulate and resolve with the indigenous people a common sense of insecurity they share in this land.

Church Position

The Church constitutes the largest Christian denomination in Fiji, most members being indigenous Fijians, and Christianity is the religion with the biggest following. This statement is issued from this position. The Methodist Church in Fiji and Rotuma wishes to make it categorically clear that its leadership is united in its condemnation of the illegal takeover of government, the destruction and looting of businesses in Suva and other parts of Fiji, the killing of a policeman and the wounding of three other people, and the general hostility directed at the Indian community. It is undivided in its support of the President and the Great Council of Chiefs in seeking a constitutional and just solution to the hostage situation and the political crisis.

Theological Responses

The Fijians being the perpetrators of these activities, the focus of this statement is on an indigenous perspective. Several theological responses may be made to the coup attempt and the lawlessness which attended this crisis. The responses relate to issues which include the following:

- the State's concern to develop multiculturalism,
- the Church theology of love and reconciliation,
- the grassroots identity question in indigenous society,

- the distinction between what is legal and what is just,
- the tension between global standards and the specific Fiji situation,
- and the nation-state in a world of transnational corporations and agencies.

Other issues may be raised from the perspectives of Indians and other groups in this nation. Of the issues listed here, the Church believes that consideration of the indigenous identity question should be given priority, and this ought to be done responsibly as part of the solution to this crisis and to light the path to Fiji's future. This immediate statement does not address all these issues.

The impoverishment and disaffection of Fijians are evident in the large number of supporters which the hostage-takers have attracted in the Parliament grounds, enabling them to create a human shield of civilians against any armed intervention by the military. If an individual breaks the law, we might be content with a psychological explanation for his deviance. When many people take part, as they have, in unlawful activities, we must look further into society for explanation.

Former Prime Minister Mahendra Chaudhry wanted his legacy to Fiji to be a substantial improvement in the standard of living of the indigenous people. But his detractors described some of his proposals as based on dishonest motives of alienating indigenous land. The depressed indigenous economic and political condition, as a commentator has noted, is not the result of 12 months of leadership by Fiji's first Indian premier. On this view, it is the result of 30 years of modern indigenous Fijian leadership which has sacrificed the economic and cultural well-being of a people for the advancement of a few. George Speight's coup attempt and the public response to it are viewed in this perspective as a symptom of complex contradictions and competing interests facing indigenous Fijian society today.

'My name is Legion; for we are many,' (Mark 5: 9) the possessed man told Jesus Christ when He asked him his name in an exorcism story from the scriptures. The man with the unclean spirit lived among the tombs; and no one could bind him any more, even with a chain. In another context, however, we are told that one exorcism may not be adequate. 'And when he comes he finds it (the house) swept and put in order. Then he goes and brings seven other spirits more evil than himself, and they enter and dwell there; and the last state of that man becomes worse than the first.' (Luke 11: 25–26)

After the first two coups in 1987, a new Constitution was promulgated in 1990 and parliamentary government reinstated. A review of that Constitution was undertaken and a fresh Constitution enacted in 1997, based on the exciting vision of a truly multicultural and dynamic society. Now, in kidnapping democratically elected Prime Minister Mahendra Chaudhry and his Cabinet, it has been said, George Speight has taken hostage of much of the hope and potential Fiji had at the turn of the century to become a nation united.

Indigenous Identity

The matter of Fijian identity is a key element which is wrapped up in the current crisis of government and the rule of law. Fijian collective consciousness is made up of the inseparable union among the three strands of *vanua* (land), *Lotu* (Church) and *Matanitu* (State). Their union is so complete that if one is affected, the whole is affected. Vanua has physical, social and cultural dimensions which are inter-related, as a local anthropologist has pointed out. It denotes the land area one is associated with, the flora and fauna, and other objects on it. It includes the social and cultural system — the people, their traditions and customs, beliefs and values, and social institutions. Its social and cultural dimensions are a source of security and confidence. It is the locality over which the ancestral spirits linger and watch over the affairs of their living descendants. For most Fijians, to part with the *vanua* is tantamount to parting with their lives.

Fijians categorise the population or inhabitants of the country, or any locality or village, into two main divisions. A person is either a *taukei* (indigene or owner) or *vulagi* (visitor or foreigner) in any place. It is a relationship of mutual obligations and clearly defined roles in which one does not count or begrudge his or her contribution to communal life. Depending on the goodwill of the people involved, it can be a gracious partnership of host and guest, or a hostile relationship of landlord and tenant.

Methodism (the *Lotu*) has contributed significantly towards improving the social life of Fijians. The missionaries, like the government, enlisted the help of chiefs in their work. The Church brought peace, unity, economic and political development. Methodism gave Fijians a written language. It pioneered Fijian education at all levels: primary, secondary, adult education, Bible schools, technical, agricultural, health and vocational education. It promoted education for girls, by setting up schools for them. The *vakatawa* (catechists) and *vakavuvuli* (teachers) took the Gospel to all comers of Fiji, so that Fijians evangelised Fijians. Even while this happened, Fijian missionaries took the Good News to the Western Pacific — Papua New Guinea, the Solomons, and what is now Vanuatu.

The close relationship between *vanua* and *Lotu* during the last one and a half centuries in Fiji has always been greatly appreciated and valued for it brought about much needed unity among the Fijian people in the early days. Their link and relative harmony helped promote civilisation and well-being in islands and villages, and continues to do so. Now the indigenous people are being challenged to reconcile global standards of human rights against the specific Fijian situation. On the one hand, there is the democratic principle of 'one man, one vote and one value' and the Christian principle of equality. On the other hand, the indigenous people have cultural values of a stratified society of chiefs and commoners, confederacies and vassal provinces, and *taukei* and *vulagi*.

Three years ago, in a public statement on the constitutional review, the Methodist Church warned indigenous leaders not to be lulled by the relative harmony their people enjoy. It said that this calm could become a new form of escape from reality if the poor, the powerless and the marginalised are not justly treated. In the developing political situation, it called on Fijian leaders to move beyond the so-called point of harmony of *vanua* and *Lotu* to address the plight of the growing number of poor and powerless Fijians.

The cleavage of the two institutions from the beginning would have been disastrous and there would not have been a Fijian race. The problem now seems to lie on the level of differentiation — in distinguishing between what is and what ought to be. The absence of such a distinction will result in the loss of a sense of direction towards the creation of community. To address this distinction must be part of the Church's contribution to the way forward for Fiji.

A PUBLIC STATEMENT BY THE PRESIDENT OF THE METHODIST CHURCH IN FIJI

Reverend Tomasi Kanailagi

Why a Public Statement?

The Methodist Church (hereinafter referred to as 'the Church') issues the following public statement, with an objective to set the record straight in regards to the stand it has chosen to take during this time of national crisis.

The Church's MANDATE is scripturally based on the teaching that our Lord Jesus Christ came not only to seek but also to save the lost, including those who are in the hands of the Devil.

In addition, the Church, as the Body of Christ and as a corporate citizen, sees an urgent need to tell its Members (approximately 250,000 in all) and the Public at large why it has taken such a stand.

How Many Sides Does the Church See?

The Church sees essentially two Parties in the current national crisis, namely :

- IMG – Interim Military Government
- GSG – the George Speight Group

However, the Church understands that there are other various groups with varying vested interests, and who are also involved, either actively or passively, in the current showdown.

Is the Church Supporting the George Speight Group?

NO, the Church IS NOT supporting the George Speight Group for the following reasons:

- The Church does not and cannot support any terrorist-type activity such as the holding of hostages for ransom at gunpoint at the parliamentary Complex.
- The Church, however, maintains contacts with the George Speight Group in matters relating to ongoing pastoral care and counselling.
- The Church has to be where its Members are to continue to be the Prophetic Voice even if it means being in the wilderness.

Is the Church Praying for the George Speight Group?

YES, the Church is praying for everyone, and during these times interceding especially on behalf of the George Speight Group, pleading before His Holy Presence to fill their lives with the love of God so that they may in turn truly love their captured hostages by setting them free to return to their homes to be with their loved ones.

Let me reiterate for the record that the Church's mandate is scripturally based on the teaching that our Lord Jesus Christ came not only to seek but also to save the lost, including those who are in the hands of the Devil.

As a matter of fact, a Delegation of the Standing Committee of the Church has on 2 June 2000 and 9 June 2000 visited Mr George Speight and his Group at the parliamentary complex, and has, among other things, pleaded with them to release the hostages at once, return all the arms and ammunition to the army, take up the Amnesty offer and join in the civil dialogue for the purpose of reshaping our united destiny.

Which Side is the Church On?

The Church is on the Interim Military Government side for the specific reasons expressed below.

- The urgent need to restore law and order since the violent and destructive events of, and since, 19 May 2000.

- The sad and fatal shooting of the late Police Constable Filipo Seavula and the destruction of Fiji TV One Station by armed thugs and violent mobs during the night of 28 May 2000.

- The impending threat on the life of His Excellency the President and Tui Nayau during the night of, and since, 29 May 2000.

- The shooting by armed gunmen from behind human shield, resulting in serious injuries sustained by three army personnel lawfully engaged in manning police checkpoints on 29 May 2000.

- The inability of the unarmed Fiji Police Force to guarantee the safety and protection of life and property against the criminal activities of the armed mob.

- The unavoidable and unfortunate decision taken by His Excellency and Tui Nayau to hand over executive authority of the State to the Republic of Fiji Military Forces.

The Church invariably believes that the Republic of Fiji Military Forces is the only legitimate institution capable of restoring law and order under the prevailing circumstances.

With respect, Ratu Timoci Silatolu of the George Speight Group has, during TV One's Close-up Program on 11 June 2000, been honest to admit that they are not capable of controlling the recent spate of violence and the ongoing criminal activities by thugs and mobs based at the parliamentary complex, notwithstanding the George Speight Group's attempts to put a stop to such criminal activities.

Further, it is the considered view of the Church that the Republic of Fiji Military Forces, and not the George Speight Group, has passed one of the legal tests accepted by judicial courts of the Commonwealth, that is to say 'a competent and effective overthrow of the existing system of government' and thus paving the way to making another Constitution.

Lest we forget, this principle very well applied to the events of 1987 and the subsequent promulgation by Decree of the 1990 Constitution of Fiji.

Indeed, the Church joins the Judiciary, the Public Service, the Police, the Business Sector and a wide cross-section of Fiji's Community, in lending its support to the Commander and Head of Government, Commodore J. Voreqe Bainimarama, MSD, JSSC, PSC.

What Mandate Would the Church Grant the RFMF?

The Church, as a corporate citizen, would, so to speak, entrust in the Interim Military Government the following mandate :

- To Restore Peace, Order and Good Government;
- To Protect Life and Property;
- To Restore Normalcy; and
- To Expedite a Quick Return to Democratic Rule for the People and by the People of Fiji.

What is the Objective of the George Speight Group?

As we understand it, the objectives sought by the George Speight Group are as follows :

- To abrogate the 1997 Constitution;
- To remove the President;
- To make a new Constitution that guarantees, inter alia, indigenous political rule; and
- To be granted Amnesty.

Has the George Speight Group Achieved their Objectives?

Yes, as we have seen and as we are assured as follows :

- The 1997 Constitution has been removed by the Interim Military Government;
- The President and Tui Nayau has effectively vacated Office;

- The Commander and Head of the Interim Military Government has assured Amnesty to Mr George Speight and the perpetrators of the armed-civilian 'coup d'état'; and

- The Commander and Head of the Interim Military Government has assured the establishment of a Constitutional Review Committee to receive public submissions, including those from the George Speight Group.

In What Way Can You Help?

The Church believes that the real solution rests with you and me, for instance:

- If you are a Chief, please request your people, if they are inside the parliamentary complex, to return home.

- If you are a parent, either mum or dad, please request your child or children, if she or he is, or they are, inside the parliamentary complex, to return home.

- If you are a wife or husband, please request your spouse, if she or he is inside the parliamentary complex, to return home.

- If you are a Priest, Minister, Deaconess, Sister, Elder, Pastor or Preacher, please request your congregation members, if they are in the parliamentary complex, to return home.

- If you are a friend, please request your friend or friends, if she or he is, or they are, inside the parliamentary complex, to return home.

- If you are an Employer, please assist by maintaining your employment within your capacity and means.

- If you are an Employee, please assist by being faithful and loyal to your Employer.

- If you are a trade unionist, please assist by pleading with your overseas counterparts to lift trade bans against our Fiji.

- If you are a responsible human being, you can help by showing love, and compassion to your fellow human beings who are in need of your immediate assistance, especially during these difficult times, irrespective of race, religion, denomination, colour or creed.

Thank You and May God Bless You All.

COUP TIMELINE
1987–2001

1987

April 11: The Labour/National Federation Party coalition defeats Ratu Sir Kamisese Mara's ruling Alliance Party in the general elections.

April 13: Coalition leader, Dr Timoci Bavadra, is sworn in as Prime Minister.

April 19: First signs of unrest emerge as Tavua villagers in the western side of Fiji set up roadblocks in protest against the new government.

April 21: About 3000 ethnic Fijians meet at Viseisei village, Lautoka, and sign a petition calling for Fijian political supremacy.

April 24: 5000 Fijian protesters march through Suva calling for the removal of the Bavadra government, saying it was Indian-dominated.

April 25: A similar march is held in Lautoka, in western Fiji.

May 14: At 10am, Lieutenant Colonel Sitiveni Ligamamada Rabuka stages the South Pacific's first military coup. He suspends the Constitution, appoints himself Commander in Chief and names a 15-member interim administration to run the country.

May 15: The Governor-General, Ratu Sir Penaia Ganilau, condemns the coup and assumes executive authority.

May 20: A group of Bavadra supporters who had gathered at Suva's Albert Park are attacked by coup supporters. Sporadic violence spreads to the greater Suva area and Nausori.

September 23: The Coalition and Alliance Party agree to form a caretaker government following the Deuba Accord initiated by Ganilau.

October 1: At 4pm, Rabuka stages his second coup, citing dissatisfaction with the Deuba Accord.

October 1: Rabuka issues two decrees formally abrogating the 1970 Constitution and sacks Ganilau.

October 6: At midnight, Rabuka formally declares Fiji a Republic, ending its ties with the Commonwealth.

December 5: Rabuka dismisses his Taukeist government and announces a 21-member mostly Alliance Cabinet. Ganilau is appointed President and Mara Prime Minister.

1988

December 5: Dr Bavadra, 55, passes away.

1990

July 24: Ganilau promulgates a new Constitution giving ethnic Fijians political supremacy.

1991

July 11: Rabuka resigns from the military to join the interim government as Deputy Prime Minister.

1992

June 28: Fiji goes to the polls. Rabuka becomes Prime Minister after the chiefs-sponsored Soqosoqo ni Vakavulewa ni Taukei party captures most of the seats.

November 30: The government budget fails after eight SVT members, led by Josefata Kamikamica, vote against it. Fresh elections are called.

1994

January 18: Mara succeeds the late Ganilau as President.

February 28: The SVT is returned to power in the general election with 31 seats. The dissident group led by Kamikamica forms the Fijian Association Party and wins three seats. The National Federation Party wins 20 seats.

1996

September 6: The Constitutional Review Commission completes a review of the 1990 Constitution. Rabuka and NFP leader Reddy had led the way for the reviews to give the country a fairer constitution.

1997

April 4: The joint Parliamentary Select Committee looking into the Reeves report agree on a multi-party executive government with 71 seats — 31 for ethnic Fijians, 27 for ethnic Indians, two for generals and one for Rotumans.

1999

May: Elections are held under the new constitution. The Labour/Party of National Unity/Fijian Association Party coalition sweeps to power. Labour wins 31 of the 71 seats. The NFP, previously the major Indian party, fails to win any seat. Rabuka's SVT wins just eight seats.

May 19: Mahendra Chaudhry is sworn in as Fiji's first non-indigenous Prime Minister after President Mara persuades the Fijian parties to support him.

2000

April 21: About 500 ethnic Fijians march through Lautoka in protest against the government. They were led by ultra-nationalist politician Apisai Tora, who had earlier revived the Taukei Movement, a Fijian pressure group.

April 28: Over 4000 Fijians stage a second protest march in Suva.

May 19: A third march by protesting Fijians attracts 10,000 people. While it is taking place, a group of armed men led by failed businessman George Speight storms Parliament and captures Chaudhry and his MPs. The drama takes place on the first anniversary of the Chaudhry government.

May 29: Establishment of an interim military government and purported abrogation of the 1997 Constitution.

July 4: A Muaniweni farmer, Chandrika Prasad, commences a legal challenge to the takeover in the High Court.

August 23: High Court hearing before judge Justice Anthony Gates.

November 15: Justice Anthony Gates ruling in Lautoka High Court. Justice Gates's judgement declares the 1997 Constitution valid.

December 15: President Ratu Sir Kamisese Mara resigns.

2001

February 19: Fiji Court of Appeal hearing commences to consider Justice Gates's November ruling contested by the interim administration.

March 1: Fiji Court of Appeal dismisses the interim administration's appeal making the following declarations in lieu of those made in the High Court:

1. The 1997 Constitution remains the supreme law of the Republic of the Fiji Islands and has not been abrogated.

2. Parliament has not been dissolved. It was prorogued on 27 May 2000 for six months.

3. The office of the President under the 1997 Constitution became vacant when the resignation of Ratu Sir Kamisese Mara took effect on 15 December 2000. In accordance with Section 88 of that Constitution, the Vice-President may perform the functions of the President until 15 March 2001 unless a President is appointed under Section 90.

SOURCES OF PREVIOUSLY PUBLISHED ARTICLES

Chapter 2 originally appeared in *The Canberra Times, The Australian* and *The Independent* (UK).

Chapter 3 originally appeared in *Pacific World*.

Chapter 5 originally appeared in the *Fiji Times*.

Chapter 6 originally appeared on Fijilive.com.

Chapter 9 originally appeared in the *Sydney Morning Herald*.

Chapter 12 originally appeared in *Eureka Street*.

Chapter 13 originally appeared in *The Listener*.

Chapter 14 originally appeared in the *Fiji Times*.

Chapter 16 originally appeared in *Pacific Journalism Online*.

Chapter 17 originally appeared in *The Listener*.

Chapter 18 originally appeared on Fijilive.com.

Chapter 19 originally appeared in the *Journal of South Pacific Law*.

Chapter 20 originally appeared in Fiji's *Daily Post*.

Chapter 21 originally appeared on *Pacific Island Report* and on the *Asia Pacific Network*.

Chapter 22 also appeared in *Pacific Economic Bulletin*.

CONTRIBUTORS

Tevita Baleiwaqa is a Research Scholar in the Division of Pacific and Asian History, Research School of Pacific and Asian Studies, The Australian National University, Canberra.

Bruce Connew is one of New Zealand's leading photo-journalists, with extensive experience in the South Pacific.

Jone Dakuvula has been an organising secretary of the Fiji Labour Party, a media adviser to ex-Prime Minister Sitiveni Rabuka, an adviser to Opposition Leader Ratu Inoke Kubuabola, and is currently with the Citizens' Constitutional Forum.

Graeme Dobell is Foreign Affairs/Defence correspondent for Radio Australia and the Australian Broadcasting Corporation. He reported on Fiji's two coups in 1987 and the seizure of the Fiji Parliament in 2000.

Roderick Ewins is working in the field of visual art and anthropology. He is currently an Honorary Research Associate at the Centre for the Arts at the University of Tasmania.

Yash Ghai is a Professor in the Faculty of Law at the University of Hong Kong and is currently chairing the Kenyan Constitutional Commission.

Usha Sundar Harris is a journalist and documentary-maker. She also lectures at the Centre for International Communication at Macquarie University in Sydney.

John D. Kelly and Martha Kaplan are anthropologists working on issues of colonisation and decolonisation in Fiji. John Kelly is an Associate Professor at the University of Chicago and Martha Kaplan holds the same position at Vassar College.

Brij V. Lal is Professor in the Division of Pacific and Asian History, Research School of Pacific and Asian Studies, The Australian National University, Canberra. He was one of the three architects of the 1997 Fiji Constitution.

Victor Lal is a former senior sub-editor on the original *Fiji Sun*, and read law at the University of Oxford, where he has held Reuters, Wingate and Research Fellowships in race and constitutionalism in multi-ethnic states. He is the author of *Fiji: Coups in Paradise*.

Hugh Laracy is Associate Professor in the Department of History at the University of Auckland where he teaches Pacific Islands History.

Vijay Mishra is a Professor of English and Comparative Literature at Murdoch University in Perth, where he writes on diasporas and postcoloniality.

Michael Pretes is a Research Scholar in the Department of Human Geography, Research School of Pacific and Asian Studies, The Australian National University, Canberra.

Sanjay Ramesh previously worked as a political analyst for the Embassy of Japan in Suva, and is currently a political editor for the Australia-based *Fiji Times*.

Mark Revington is a staff writer for New Zealand's *The Listener* magazine.

Mere Tuisalalo Samisoni is a Fijian entrepreneur and businesswoman, and the founder and managing director of Hot Bread Kitchen. She is active in women's and health issues in Fiji.

Sir Vijay R. Singh is a Barrister of the High Courts of England, Australia and Fiji, and a former Speaker of the House of Representatives, Fiji.

Daryl Tarte is the former head of the Fiji Sugar Industry Tribunal and the independent chairman of Fiji's Media Council. He is also the author of several novels and commentaries on Fijian issues.

Teresia Teaiwa is a Lecturer in Pacific Studies at the Victoria University of Wellington, New Zealand.

Phil Thornton is a journalist with the Australian Centre for Independent Journalism investigating human rights abuses in Fiji.

Christine Weir is a Research Scholar in the Division of Pacific and Asian History, Research School of Pacific and Asian Studies, The Australian National University, Canberra.

Taina Woodward is an Indigenous Fijian active in women's issues.